THE HEART OF LONDON

THE HEART OF LONDON

BY

H. V. MORTON

An ever-muttering prisoned storm,
The heart of London beating warm:
JOHN DAVIDSON, "Ballads and Songs"

THIRTEENTH EDITION

METHUEN & CO. LTD.
36 ESSEX STREET W.C.
LONDON

First Published	.	.	.	.	June 11th	*1925*
Second Edition	.	.	.	.	January	*1926*
Third Edition	.	.	.	.	April	*1926*
Fourth Edition (Illustrated)	.	.	.	October	*1926*
Fifth Edition	.	.	.	.	October	*1926*
Sixth Edition.	.	.	.	.	February	*1928*
Seventh Edition	.	.	.	.	December	*1928*
Eighth Edition	.	.	.	.	May	*1929*
Ninth Edition	.	.	.	.	December	*1929*
Tenth Edition	.	.	.	.	June	*1930*
Eleventh Edition (Illustrated)	.	.	January	*1931*
Twelfth Edition	.	.	.	.	January	*1931*
Thirteenth Edition	.	.	.	.		*1931*

PRINTED IN GREAT BRITAIN

To
S. D. W.

CONTENTS

The Heart of London

Contents

The Heart of London

LONDON'S GROWTH

Here Herbs did grow
And Flowers sweet
But now 'tis called
Saint George's Street.

—An 18th century inscription on a
London tavern

NOTE TO THE THIRD EDITION

THESE essays were written day after day, week after week, to keep pace with the relentless machines of the "Daily Express." Since this book was published many kind unknown friends have written to tell me that here they have found something that is London; but they should not thank me: they should thank the great city which, written to death generation by generation, is an undying topic, discovered age by age is still inexhaustible; stripped bare of mystery by many writers has never lost its magic.

H. V. M.

London

*When a man is tired of London he is tired
of life : for there is in London all that life
can afford*

—Dr. Johnson

THE
HEART OF LONDON

The New Romance ⚬ ⚬ ⚬ ⚬

WHEN eight million men and women decide
to live together on the same spot things are
bound to happen.

London, in lineal descent from Thebes and
Rome, is one of those queer massings together of
humanity which Civilization dumps on a small
plot of earth before handing the lease of Destiny,
not knowing whether to laugh or cry about it.
Great cities are strange inevitable phenomena.
It is wrong to compare them with hives, for in a
hive the wish of the individual has been sacrificed
unquestioningly to the good of the community.
Had we ascended from the bee perhaps the
greatest happiness we could achieve would be an
unspectacular death in the service of the London
County Council.   But in London, as in all modern
cities, it is the individual who counts.   Our eight
millions split themselves up into ones and twos :
little men and little women dreaming their private
dreams, pursuing their own ambitions, crying
over their own failures, and rejoicing at their own
successes.

Fear built the first cities.   Men and women
herded behind a wall so that they might be safe.

The Heart of London

Then came trade ; and cities grew into lucky bags in which men dipped for profit. Essentially they remain lucky bags to this day. London's millions pour into London and carry off their loot every Friday ; but that, thank heaven, is not the whole story. A city develops Tradition and Pride. London has greater tradition and pride than any other city in the world.

So when I ask myself why I love London I realize that I appreciate that ancient memory which is London—a thing very like family tradition for which we in our turn are responsible to posterity—and I realize that I am every day of my life thrilled, puzzled, charmed, and amused by that flood-tide of common humanity flowing through London as it has surged through every great city in the history of civilization. Here is every human emotion. Here in this splendid theatre the comedy and the tragedy of the human heart are acted day and night. Love and treachery, beauty and ugliness, laughter and tears chase one another through the streets of London every minute of the day, often meeting and mixing in the strangest fashion, because London is just a great mass of human feeling, and Man, never clearly labelled " Hero " or " Villain " as in melodrama, is capable of so much moral complexity that you might almost say that good and bad exist in him at the same moment.

Had I been born a few thousand years ago I feel sure that I could have written much the same book about Thebes or Babylon, because the only things that change radically in life are fashions

The New Romance

and inventions. The human heart was patented long ago and the Creator has not seen fit to bring out a later model.

After dinner one night a woman fixed large eyes on me and confided that in a previous incarnation she had been Cleopatra. She was my tenth Cleopatra. She told me that there was no romance in modern life, and, looking a little withdrawn as if remembering some Alexandrian indiscretion, she said : " No surprise, no—you know what I mean ? —no real poetry."

I always think it best not to argue with queens ; but I believe that the surprise, the romance, and the poetry of a modern city are fiercer than they were in the past. The drama of the ancient autocracies was played with so small a cast. The rest was suffering. People with large eyes were never in their past lives anything less than queens or princes, and thus their naturally vivid memories of a small and brilliant circle dim a recollection of the dumb majority beneath their wills. In spite of the supply of desirable lamps in Bagdad the census of owner-drivers must have been quite negligible, so that the average inhabitant must have lived through the romance of those days sitting in the same patch of sun, bitten by insects and trodden on by negroes.

In London, and in the free cities of this modern world, the drama of life widens, the characters increase and the unchanging human heart, no happier perhaps in the long run, beats less timorously than it did, yet leaping in sympathy to the same old loves and fears and hates.

The Heart of London

Every day our feelings vibrate to some stray unimportance. Life is full of portentous triviality. Is it not strange that our minds often refuse to recognize some sensation—a word like a worn-out boot—while they react immediately to something so small as to be almost foolish ? You may be bored stiff by the front page of the evening paper, but you go home remembering some common thing seen or heard ; some little humanity : the sight of a man and a girl choosing a child's cot, two people saying good-bye at a street corner, the quiet hatred in a man's eyes— or the love. . . .

Let us now go out into London.

Where the Eagles Sleep   ⁀   ⁀   ⁀

ONE o'clock in the City of London. Crowds overflow the pavement into the narrow, twisting road. Young men in striped trousers, ruled like ledgers, black coats sober as a bill of lading, rush or saunter, according to their natures, towards a quick lunch-bar, where a girl with golden hair will give them beer and mutton. Girls, arm-in-arm, discuss those eternal verities— dress, love, and another woman—as they go primly or coyly, according to their nature, towards two poached eggs and a cup of tea. Here and there a large man in a silk hat, who may be a millionaire or a bankrupt, chases the inevitable chop. And the traffic roars, throbs, and thunders.

But behind a tall hoarding that shouts dog-matically of soap and shirts and pills things are quiet. Out of the chaos a great new bank will rise. Workmen sit around in picturesque groups eating. On their knees are spotted handkerchiefs in which lie gigantic sandwiches cut by wives in the early dawn. They carve them with clasp-knives and carry them to their mouths, the clasp-knives upright in their hands grazing their cheeks. They drink from tin cans, and wonder, in rich monosyllables, " wot " will win the three-thirty.

I stand on the edge of a vast pit in which, down through successive strata—brick, tiles, black earth, powdered cement—lies the clay on which London rests. It is a deep, dark hole. It is as if some surgeon, operating on the great body of the city, has bared it to the spine. I look down with awe at the accumulation of nearly two thousand years of known history piled, layer on layer, twenty-four feet above the primal mud.

How amazing to gaze down into that pit where the marvellous record of London lies clear as layers of cream in a cake: Victorian, Georgian, Stuart, Plantagenet, Norman, Anglo-Saxon, and Roman. There it stops, for there it began. Below, nothing but mud and ooze, hundreds of thousands of years of unrecorded Time, century after century written in mud, forest after forest, springing up, dying, falling into decay; and who knows what awful drama of great creatures struggling in green undergrowth and river slime long before the first man climbed a tree on Ludgate Hill and looked round fearfully on that which was not yet London?

A workman clambers into the pit, prods around with a stick, and shouts up to his mate:

" Hi, Bill, here's a bit more ! "

And pat-pat-pat on the parapet fall hard, encrusted fragments that look like flat cakes of sealing wax. I pick them up, knock off the caked earth, and find a beautiful little fragment of deep red pottery, one the rim of a delicate vase, another the rounded base of a little cup, and in the bottom something is written: " Fl. Germanus. F." Just that.

What does it mean? It means that I have seen the deep roots of London pulled up, the roots that go right back to Rome. "Fl. Germanus. F." is the trade mark of Flavius Germanus, a

Where the Eagles Sleep

potter who lived in the time of the Cæsars, and
" F " stands for " Fecit," meaning " Flavius
Germanus made it." What a message to receive
in modern London behind a hoarding advertising
pills, while the traffic roars, throbs, and thunders !

* * *

Every week a sackful of Rome is dug up in the
City of London when a new bank is built. For
we stand on the shoulders of Rome. Men from
the London and the Guildhall Museums watch
the excavations like lynxes, collect the little bits
of red pottery, the coins, the bits of green and
mauve glass, this wreckage of that first London ;
that far-flung limb of Rome crowning its single
hill.

* * *

As I stand there, so modern, such a parvenu,
an omnibus ticket still stuck in the strap of my
wrist-watch, I hold the cup of Flavius. What
do I see ? I see the first London and its colonists
pegging out their camp. Then Boudicca, blood,
fire, a ruin. The second London rises from the
smoke, a London old enough to have a story to
tell the young men ; and round this London they
are building a wall.

Gradually, as a vision in a crystal clears and
forms out of mist, I see a smaller, colder Rome
standing with its marble feet in Thames water.
I see rows of wood and red-tile houses running
within the walls in straight lines like tents within

The Heart of London

a castrum; I see the marble capitals under our grey skies, the majestic circular sweep of the theatre, the white gleam of the Forum, the gates with their statues, the baths at the gates, the long straight streets crowded, noisy, varied. I see the shaggy Britons and the Gauls move to a side as the Roman troops come clattering over the stones, their helmets shining, swords at hips; the marvellous short sword that carved out an Empire as a girl might cut a cake.

And the heart of this little English Rome, how did it beat? I imagine that it knew the enterprising business man opening up new markets, the enthusiastic soldier always dreaming of sending the Eagles north, the inevitable Phœnician with his galley at the docks and his shop somewhere in the city, the bad boy sent to colonial London to expiate, and women making the best of it, always three months behind Rome in fashion: wives and sweethearts who had followed their men into barbary. O, the homesickness and heroism of colonization! How many old men must have wept to see their careful vines wilt in the London clay; and I wonder if Londinium Augusta numbered among its inhabitants the optimistic gardener who bored his friends with a vision of olives in a neat Italian row!

There would come a time in this first London when a small boy would say to his mother: " Tell me about Rome! "

And she would sit facing the broad Thames, talking of Italy as a homesick woman in Winnipeg might talk of England:

8

Where the Eagles Sleep

" Do you see those galleys coming up under the bridge like water beetles ? They come from Ostia—from Rome. They bring soldiers and— sometimes people go home in them ! Yes, dear, perhaps when you grow up you too will go. The sun always shines there, and it is seldom cold as it is here. When your father was a little boy like you . . ."

So the tale would go on.

Then I see the market-place, the marvellous mixture of race which Rome drew to her cities : the dark Iberian soldier pressed into service for duty on the Wall, the Gaul, the German, the negro, the merchants with their wares, the amber from the Baltic, the pearls, the perfumes from the East, the brown fingers holding out gold chains as the Roman ladies go by. . . .

What chatter of a six months old scandal as the women walk to the baths ; what discussion of Rome's latest *coiffure*, her newest pin, her smartest sandal ! At the docks the creak of timber and the straining of a released rope, the " one, two, three " as the oarsmen dip their great blades in the Thames ; and a galley goes home with letters to Cæsar from the Governor of London.

Londinium Augusta ! There is nothing between her and Verulamium but a straight road through the forest, then another road, more forests, and proud Camulodunum on its hill. Three fortified islands in a green sea. So England takes shapes out of the mists of Time ; so London begins.

And I like to think, to round off the picture,

9

that, on a cold night of winter, when brittle green stars glitter in the sky like glass, some grey old wolf creeps to the edge of the Hampstead woods and licks his jaws as he looks towards the first lights of London. Then he yawns and blinks his eyes as a dog blinks and looks away from something he does not understand. So he trots softly among the trees with the instinct that things are different; that—something has happened to the Hill!

Oriental ∘ ∘ ∘ ∘ ∘ ∘

A YOUNG girl with eyes like the fish-pools of Heshbon sits outside a butcher's shop on an upturned crate. Her fingers are covered in rings, and when she laughs she throws back her fuzzy head, exposing her plump, olive-coloured throat, as Moons of Delight have been doing throughout the history of the Orient.

She is beautiful after her kind. In five more years, however, she will look like a side-show. Her lithe grace, her round face, her firm, white neck will be submerged in regrettable tissue. The eye passing over her façade will find it impossible to excavate her recent beauty. She will be like a thin girl who somehow has been merged with a fat woman. She will be "herself with yesterday's ten thousand years,"—and yesterday winning all along the line. That is the burden of the Jewess.

However, at the moment she is ripe as a peach is ripe before it falls naturally into the hand. Were I a Sultan, swaying above the street in a litter, I would roll a lazy eye in her direction, make a minute movement of a jewelled finger, and, later at the palace, I would address her:

"Moon of Great Beauty and Considerable Possibility," I would say, "whither comest thou, O Radiance, and who is thy father?"

Whereupon she would spit at me with her eyes and reply:

The Heart of London

"Cancher see I'm respectable . . . cancher?
You're a nice chep, you are, sitting up there
dressed like a dorg's dinner and talkin' like thet
. . . lemme go . . ."

For though her eyes are the eyes of Ruth among
the alien corn, her larynx is that of Bill Sykes.
The street in which she sits, shedding this varied
atmosphere, is lined on either side by a row of
rough booths. It is a mere track between two
bright hedges of merchandise. Here the fruit-
sellers expose their pyramids of red-gold oranges,
their African plums, their pineapples; there the
sellers of shoes wait patiently beneath their
pendulous racks. The sellers of cloth walk up
and down with bright, stabbing colours, daringly
mixed, slung across their shoulders, and the drink
merchants, with their cooling brews—never absent
from an Oriental market—stand beside their
ample golden globes.

Through this lane of bright colour moves the
crowd—the women young, straight, and mostly
beautiful in a dark, passionate way; the old
women fat and round; the men sallow, bearded,
and incredibly wrinkled. Among them crowd the
abject creatures so well known in the East, who
clutch a handful of vegetables or three inferior
lemons with which they try to undersell the regular
merchants.

Where is it? It might be Cairo, Bagdad,
Jerusalem, Aleppo, Tunis, or Tangier, but, as a
matter of fact, it is Petticoat Lane in Whitechapel
—a penny ride from Ludgate Hill!

As I walked through Petticoat Lane I thought

that if we had a sunny climate this part of White-chapel would become one of the famous show-places of the world. Here you have the East without its lepers, without small-pox, without the flies, without the impertinent stinks. This is the scene of rich and amusing variety which, were it only a few thousand expensive miles from London, under a blue sky, would attract the attention of the artist and the traveller.

The attitude towards commerce is as old as barter. I saw a neatly bearded woman, whose brown coat looked as though it was draped over a barrel, go up to a fishmonger, standing beside two gigantic codfish and a number of smaller fish.

" How much ? " asked the woman, indicating a nice group of still life.

" Six shillings," replied the fishmonger, with a keen glance from small, black eyes.

" One and ten," remarked the woman, reflect-ively turning a plaice upside down and prodding it with a fat finger.

Whereupon a singular change took place in the fishmonger's aloof attitude. He was insulted, outraged. Suddenly, picking up a plaice by the tail, he said with a threatening gesture :

" I'll wipe it acrost yeh face ! "

The customer was not outraged as a woman would have been in Oxford Street ; she just shrugged her fat shoulders, as she would have done in Damascus, and moved away, knowing full well that before she had retreated very far she would be recalled—as she was. After a brisk argument she bought the fish for two and fourpence and they parted friends!

I have seen exactly the same drama played on a carpet in Alexandria.

*　　*　　*

What strange foreign eatables you see here: vile-looking messy dishes, anæmic cucumbers, queer salted meats, varied sausages of East European origin, the inevitable onion, and, of course, olives. Smoked salmon has customers at ten shillings a pound.

But the people are more interesting than their surroundings or their food. Such gnarled, lined faces, such live eyes, such a patriarchal air. That is the old orthodox generation. The new? Such smartish young semi-Englishmen prospering in trade on an education for which the old generation has starved itself. They can pronounce their w's and their th's. They have an eye on Hampstead or even on the Golden West. The daughters of Israel, powdered and rouged, flit with their dark, and often alluring, eyes from dressmaker's shop to dressmaker's shop, pert and self-assured, well dressed even in their working clothes.

This rift between the old and the new generations is the first thing that strikes you. There seem several hundred years between them. What tragedies does it conceal, what human stories? Many an old man nodding over his crowded counter has sent a son to the 'varsity. This is not fiction, and those will not believe it who do not understand that Israel has always given over its heart to its children. If the elements of domestic tragedy are not here, where are they ?— for Israel, scattered in its wanderings and oppressed, never lost the Tables of the Law, never forgot the old things, never became quite deaf to the sounds of tents in a wind ; but now the old men can say to their children : " My thoughts are not your thoughts, neither are your ways my ways."

*　　*　　*

In a narrow street full of jewellers' shops I saw a bent old patriarch gazing into a window at a nine-branched candlestick ; on the opposite side of the road came a young girl in her sand-coloured silk stockings and her tight black coat, swinging a silver bag—very far from the flocks and herds was she ! Again I saw a limousine stop at a tiny shop. An old woman ran out, a young man leapt from the car to meet her, and when he kissed her there was joy shining in her eyes. Joseph ? The modern Prodigal Son ?

*　　*　　*

I caught a penny omnibus back to England with the feeling that I might have spent two hundred pounds and seen less of the East, less of romance, and much less of life.

Ships Come Home ✦ ✦ ✦ ✦

IN the grey dawn liners from the Seven Seas slip into the docks of London; and men and women gather there to meet friends. Some even meet their sweethearts. They are the lucky ones.

It was not yet light. Dawn was a good hour away, and it was very cold. I was travelling away from London towards Woolwich in a jangling, dirty workman's train. On the platform at Fenchurch Street I had noticed several other people obviously on their way to meet friends, but they had been assimilated in the gloom of the long train; and I was glad, for I was enjoying myself in a carriage full of dock workers: a carriage that reeked of smoke and manly conversation. The train ploughed wearily on through the darkness, stopping at stations. . . . Stepney East. . . . Burdett Road. . . . Bromley. . . . Canning Town. . . . Bleak, unfriendly places under their pale lights. More early Londoners stormed the carriage at each station and split pleasantries rather like roadmen hitting a spike:

" Goo' mornin', Bill. . . ."

" It ain't a goo' mornin'. It's a blinkin' cold mornin' ! "

The laughter could not have been louder if the retort had been made by a judge or a king !

The conversation was both technical and sporting. The technical discussion centred round the life and shortcomings of a certain foreman, who,

Ships Come Home

I gathered, although he knew less about a ship than a —— —— school-teacher, was, if not a man of iron, at least a man of blood. So they said. Football and racing! They knew the parentage, habits, and hobbies of every League player, also the result of contests going right back to ancient times. They all had " a bit " on the three-thirty.

*   *   *

North Woolwich! In the still air of dawn I could feel the nearness of shipping. I could not see much, but I knew that I was surrounded by ships. The docks were not awake. The steam winches were not screaming, the hammers were stilled; yet over the dark docks lay the presence of great ships home from sea. . . .

I walked on past the shrouded cranes, standing in their straight lines near the water's side. I came upon a tall ship looming up like a cliff. I could make out a man leaning over her deck far above. I asked him if this was the ship I wanted. He opened his mouth, and there descended curious, unwilling sounds, like something trying hard to escape from his throat and then changing its mind and trying to get back again. I think he was talking Japanese.

So I walked along to the stern of the ship to read the name, and there I met a man gazing upward, too. It turned out that we were both looking for the same ship, so we walked on together.

" What an experience it is," he said. " I wonder how many people in London have ever done this. I'm generally asleep at this time of the morning. How early London wakes up. Think of those workmen's trains. . . ."

" Are you meeting a friend in the ——," I asked.

He coughed slightly and said, " Yes," and the way he said it told me that it was going to be a romantic occasion.

Then dawn. If there is anything more wonderful in London than dawn coming up over the tangled shipping of the docks I would like to know of it. First a silvery light in the air, a chilly greyness, then a flush in the east, and with startling suddenness every mast, every funnel, every leaning crane is silhouetted jet-black against the pearl-coloured sky. . . . Unreal . . . still . . . silent.

Gradually the docks awaken. Men walk along the wharfside, doors are opened. In the depths of little ships men rise and become busy with ropes ; there is, from some, a smell of frying bacon ; on tall ships mast lights grow pale in the dawn light, men in swinging cradles yawn and start painting a ship's hull, and from far off sounds the first hammer of a new day.

As light grows one's sense of smell increases. This is strange. The air is now full of a pungent smell of hemp and tow and tar, and even distant docks, stored with their merchandise, seem to contribute their part as the dawn wind blows.

High up in the sky there is a flush of pink cloud, such a delicate flamingo pink that changes, spreads, and fades even as you look. It becomes gold, and you know that at any moment the sun may rise up like a tocsin and call all the world to work.

*   *   *

We found the ship. A mountain she was, towering up above us with tiny holes in her side like the entrances to caves. She smelt of fried fish, bacon and eggs and coffee. . . .

Soon after I was aboard I had to look the other way for I had seen my friend holding a girl in his arms and I had heard him say:

"And how are you, darling?"

"Splendid!" she cried. "Let me look at you! Come into the light."

So you see wonderful things happen to some people when tall ships come out of the Seven Seas and find their way to London Town.

Treasure Trove ✦ ✦ ✦ ✦ ✦

SOME things, such as umbrellas, suitcases, trousers, boots, bedsteads, and hats, both male and female, can become so old that it would be a decency could they disintegrate and vanish into thin air. Nothing can be quite so old and dissipated as an umbrella. But, no ; the effortless Nirvana which these things have earned is denied them ; they are spread out on the cobbles of the Caledonian Market (North London) every Friday, in the hope that their pitiful pilgrimage may continue.

When I walked into this remarkable once-a-week junk-fair I was deeply touched to think that any living person could need many of the things displayed for sale. For all round me, lying on sacking, were the driftwood and wreckage of a thousand lives : door knobs, perambulators in *extremis*, bicycle wheels, bell wire, bed knobs, old clothes, awful pictures, broken mirrors, unromantic china goods, gaping false teeth, screws, nuts, bolts, and vague pieces of rusty iron, whose mission in life, or whose part and portion of a whole, Time had obliterated.

It seemed that all the queer things in all the little shops in London's by-streets had been poured out in a last desperate effort of salesmanship, while on every hand, above the Oriental clamour of stall-holders and the negative remarks of the public, rose the all-prevailing cry :

Treasure Trove

" Come on, ma, take it for sixpence . . . four-pence ? . . . twopence ? All right, then I'll *give* it you. . . ."

I must say, however, that I never observed this threat carried into execution.

As I walked between the aisles of junk I remembered the story of a friend who went to this market out of curiosity, and came away unexpectedly in a taxicab with a priestess. He had bought a mummy for ten shillings. And well can I believe it. I longed for something like this to happen to me, for that is how life should go. When you look forward to a thing, or search for it and find it, you are invariably disappointed because your mind has had time to experience it and possess it and tire of it long before it comes. But the joy of sudden, unexpected things seldom fails. I have always envied J., not his priestess, because she smelt like a French third-class carriage and had to be buried at night, but his meeting with her. That must have been wonderful. He was walking along thinking about door knobs or bell wire when he saw her : " My God, a mummy ! Man or woman ? Woman ! How romantic ! Probably she was beautiful and young ! She used to shake a sistrum at Karnak beside the Nile and wear a lovely pleated skirt and nothing underneath. . . ."

For a second, perhaps two—anyhow just long enough to hand over a ten-shilling note—I think he loved her as much as you can love a mummy, and although his affection waned in Bloomsbury when he had to help her out of the taxi, it must have been worth it just for the sharp delirium of that meeting—he ardent, romantic; she a bit glazed and fish-like in more ways than one, but eternally feminine, though, as it were, canned.

I walked on trying not to expect that anything so wonderful would come my way. Near the entrance a man offered me someone's skeleton for seven-and-sixpence, and when I said " No " he put down the box in which it is kept and remarked to his wife : " Now, don't put your foot through the skull, Emma." At the next stall a young mother was buying a cradle festooned in dusty black lace.

I watched a man buy three dentist's door plates for three and sixpence, and the dealer generously threw in a bowler hat that looked like the hero of a hundred brawls.

Then, here and there among the dense, moving crowds of women in search of cheap saucepans, and those odd lengths of cloth which women of all classes accumulate, I saw the dealers from the more fashionable districts looking for something for five shillings to sell later in the West End for five pounds. There were also numbers of treasure-seekers, men and women—smart, well dressed— collectors of antiques, nosing round like setters for Chippendale chairs, Japanese prints, Chinese jade, and Queen Anne silver.

Half the collectors in London make it a point to visit this place every Friday in search of loot; and they walk round like pirate Kings ready to pounce on the instant.

Most curious and sad to look upon were the old

shoes, poor down-at-heel, crinkly-toed things, standing dressed by the right on their last parade, some with a remote Jermyn Street look about them, others all that remains of someone's ancient corn-ridden aunt. Among a pile of boots which looked as though they had walked every yard of the road to ruin, I saw, tall and upright, a pair of women's riding boots, proud still in their decline. I also saw a pair of gold dance-slippers, somehow naked and ashamed.

A large woman was turning this way and that a slim little bride's dress with the faded orange blossom still sewn on it. A white veil went with it, gashed and torn. The fat woman moved on, lured by a decayed washstand, and onward still to flirt a moment with an old brass bedstead. I saw other hands—big coarse hands—pulling this forgotten little bride's dress about, pawing it. What a pity it could not melt away and save itself from this supreme insult!

*　　*　　*

In a corner lying on a sack I saw an Egyptian antiquity. I pounced!

" How much ? "

A young man answered me with an Oxford accent.

" Fifteen shillings, sir."

I wondered what on earth this superior person was doing there standing back behind a sack spread with antiques. Was it his hobby, or was it a bet ?

" I think," went on the Oxford voice, " you

will agree with me that the hieroglyphs were added at a later period. Perhaps during the Ptolemaic age, though I think the figure is much older, possibly Eighteenth Dynasty."

I was astonished to hear this in the Caledonian Market.

" No, indeed, sir, I do not do this for fun: I do it for bread and butter. Since the war, you know! Yes; I make enough to live. I have a *flair* for antiques. I buy cheaply and sell reasonably, and collectors always come to me."

Strange spot, the Caledonian Market!

As I went out I was offered another skeleton for ten shillings.

Cenotaph ◊ ◊ ◊ ◊ ◊ ◊

TEN-THIRTY A.M. in Whitehall on a cold, grey February morning.

There is expectancy at the Horse Guards, where two living statues draped in scarlet cloaks sit their patient chargers. A group of sightsers wait at the gates for the high note of a silver cavalry trumpet, for the click of hoofs on the cobbles, and a shining cavalcade beneath an arch, the pageantry that precedes that silent ceremony of changing a guard that " turns out " for no man but the King.

Laden omnibuses go down to Westminster or up to Charing Cross, and as they pass every passenger looks at the two Life Guards in their scarlet glory, for they are one of the sights of London that never grows stale. Taxicabs and limousines spin smoothly left and right, men and women enter and leave Government offices : a Whitehall morning is moving easily, leisurely, elegantly, if you like, towards noon.

I walk on to Westminster, and in the centre of the road, cream-coloured, dominant, stands the Cenotaph.

*   *   *

More than six years ago the last shot was fired. Six years. It is long enough for a heart to become convalescent. Sharp agonies which at the time of their happening seem incapable of healing have a merciful habit of mending in six years. A broken love-affair that turned the world into a pointless waste of Time has ended in a happy marriage in six years. A death that left so much unspoken, so much regret, so much to atone for, falls in six years into its pathetic perspective a little nearer Nineveh and Tyre.

I look up at the Cenotaph. A parcels delivery boy riding a tricycle van takes off his worn cap. An omnibus goes by. The men lift their hats. Men passing with papers and documents under their arms, attaché and despatch cases in their hands—all the business of life—bare their heads as they hurry by.

Six years have made no difference here. The Cenotaph—that mass of national emotion frozen in stone—is holy to this generation. Although I have seen it so many times on that day once a year when it comes alive to an accompaniment of pomp as simple and as beautiful as church ritual, I think that I like it best just standing here in a grey morning, with its feet in flowers and ordinary folk going by, remembering.

*   *   *

I look up to Charing Cross and down to Westminster. On one side Whitehall narrows to a slit, against which rises the thin, black pencil of the Nelson column ; on the other Westminster Abbey, grey and devoid of detail, seems etched in smoke against the sky, rising up like a mirage from the silhouette of bare trees.

The wind comes down Whitehall and pulls the flags, exposing a little more of their red, white, and

blue, as if invisible fingers were playing with them.
The plinth is vacant. The constant changing
trickle of a crowd that later in the day will stand
here for a few moments has not arrived. There
is no one here.

No one? I look, but not with my eyes, and I
see that the Empire is here: England, Canada,
Australia, New Zealand, South Africa, India . . .
here—springing in glory from our London soil.

* * *

In a dream I see those old mad days ten years
ago. How the wind fingers the flags. . . .

I remember how, only a few weeks ago, as a
train thundered through France, a woman sitting
opposite to me in the dining car said, " The
English ! " I looked through the window over
the green fields, and saw row on row, sharply white
against the green, rising with the hill and dropping
again into the hollows—keeping a firm line as they
had been taught to do—a battalion on its last
parade.

The Cenotaph and no one there? That can
never be.

* * *

Look ! Near the mottled white and black of
the War Office far up Whitehall is a platoon of
Guardsmen marching. As they come near I see
that they are men of the Irish Guards. They
swing their arms and stride out, carrying their
rifles at a perfect " slope." They are very young,
the " eighteen-year-olds " we used to call them in

1918 when they were called up to form the " young soldiers' battalions." I remember how frightened some of them were at this thing that had happened to them, and how often, when one was orderly officer padding round at night, a boy soldier would be crying like a child in the darkness at some harshness or in a wave of homesickness.

The old recipe has worked with the Guards ! On they come, a platoon of tough Irish soldiers, their solemn faces grim and set under their peaked caps, their belts snow white with pipeclay.

They approach the Cenotaph :

" Platoon ! " roars the sergeant. " Eyes—right ! "

He slaps his rifle butt, and the heads swing round.

" Eyes—front ! "

* * *

The Cenotaph stands there with a wind pulling . . . pulling like fingers touching the Flag.

Romance on Wheels ∽   ∾   ∾   ∾

WHEN normal London folk have gone home
to bed the coffee-stalls come trundling out
of the mysterious dark to stay at street corners
and bridge-heads till the dawn. Ask your friends
if they have ever sought refreshment at a coffee-
stall. I wager that perhaps only the Bad Boy of
the Family or Dance Club Jane have experienced
the happiness of sausages at 3 A.M. in this temple
of romance.

The coffee-stall at the street corner is the only
thing left in our modern world that approximates
to the mediæval inn or guest-house. Hotels are
graded and standardized, and you know exactly
the kind of people you will find in them. Good
hotels are so much alike that patrons often have
to ask the hall porter whether they are in London
or Rome.

But the little coffee-stall, set netwise at street
corners to catch queer fish, is dramatic. If ever
I write a play the first act will take place round
a coffee-stall; but I am told that this has been
done ; and no wonder. Here it is that you, like
some traveller in the old days before the last
dragon died, will meet varlets and squires, knights
on some bright errantry, damsels in distress, and
many a wandering fool : all the old characters of
Romance like moths round a flame, dropping in
out of the night to snatch a sausage and then off,
mysterious, elusive, into the night.

The Heart of London

There was a mist round the coffee-stall when I found it : one of those strange, fugitive fogs that drift like ghosts at night in the hollows. In the mist the stall was a glow-worm, yellow and furry, warm and desirable, a home to wanderers and fly-by-nights, comforting with its smell of hot coffee and its pungent, inviting sizzle.

Six or seven people, black against the yellowness and the banked Woodbines and the tiers of depressing cakes, gazed round suspiciously as I came in out of the incalculable dark, for after a certain time of morning every plain man may have the mark of the devil on him. Round this stall were the following people :

A young man with a silk hat on the back of his head and a white evening scarf hanging over a white shirt front.

A young girl with yellow, shingled hair and a pair of silver dance-shoes peeping out from under a moleskin cloak.

A very arch young woman, who was making hopeless eyes at the young man in the silk hat out of sheer enthusiasm, as she ground cigarette stump after cigarette stump into her saucer.

Three or four workmen from neighbouring road repairs.

Two men holding little black bags, who may have been telephone officials, burglars, printers, disguised peers, or returning prodigal sons, but mostly they looked like uncles from Balham.

From the young man in the silk hat I eaves-dropped that everything was " topping " and that Millie was " awfully struck " on Arthur, and from his pretty partner I gathered that coffee and buns at 3 A.M. were awfully good fun, and that she had sprung a ladder in her stocking.

" By why," she asked, " are coffee-stalls licensed to sell stamps ? "

The arch young woman looked up swiftly, and said all in one breath :

" So that men can write home and tell their wives why they were kept late at the office. Who's going to stand me a coffee ? "

No one laughed ; then, surprisingly, one of the solemn Balham uncles put down the money and as solemnly went on talking to his companion about horses. The arch lady turned her back on them, drank her coffee, borrowed a broken mirror, rouged her lips, said, " Well, cheerio, all ! " and vanished, archly.

A taxicab driver arrived with a clatter, excavated threepence from that deep remoteness where all taxicab drivers keep their money, and departed with the young man and the young woman. The Balham uncles went off with a non-committal air, which made me wonder whether they were off to break into a house or off home to sleep beneath a scriptural text.

" All sorts, sir, I gets here," said the coffee-stall man as he sloshed about among the dirty plates. " You remember that cat burglar, him what broke into Grosvenor Gardens the other night ? I've had him 'ere. 'Safact ! Talkin' to a reel lord, he was, too ! Yes ; I get a lord now and again, but they ain't no different from ordinary people. They eats their sausages like everybody else and leaves the gristle like everybody else and only puts tuppence under the saucer. Why, you might be a lord for all I know——"

He paused, then in case I might get proud and haughty he added :

" Or a cat burglar. . . . Well, as I was sayin', up comes this 'ere cat burglar, smart as you like, puts a little black bag where your leanin' now— full of jools it was, but I didn't know—and he asks for a cup of coffee and a barth bun. He chips into the conversation and talks to 'is lordship quite the gentleman. ' Nice chap that,' says 'is nibs after he'd gone. ' What is he ? ' ' I dunno.' I tell him ; and at that moment up run a couple of coppers, all hot and bothered. " 'Ave you seen a dark young man wearin' a blue double-breasted suit, height five foot ten and a narf and of a pale complexion ? ' ' Thousands,' I says, going on wiping up ; I could see something was up and I wasn't splitting. Then they told me about 'im, and I told them about 'im, and off they ran like a couple of ferrets. Catch him ? Not likely. . . . Good morning, sir ! "

Suddenly into the circle of light stepped a man carrying a cat that had been born white. A thin, melancholy cat and a thin, melancholy man, middle-aged, rain-coated, and grim. He placed the thin cat on the oilcloth counter, and the man behind at once poured out a saucer of milk.

The cat slunk to it guiltily. The man watched it as if he had never seen a cat before, and stroked its back. Then he buttoned it inside his raincoat and went away.

Romance on Wheels

" Collects cats, he does," said the coffee-stall man, as he banged about among his unwashed china. " Says they follow him. Most nights he comes along with a stray cat, buys it milk, takes it home and looks after it. Regular walkin' cats' home, he is. . . . Good morning, sir . . ."

Round the bend of the road swung the first gold tramcar of a new day.

Ghosts of the Fog ✿ ✿ ✿ ✿

FOG in London.

Men are like flat figures cut in black paper. All things become two-dimensional. Carts, motor-cars, omnibuses are shadows that nose their way painfully like blind beasts. The fog has a flavour. Many flavours. At Marble Arch I meet a delicate after-taste like melon ; at Ludgate Hill I taste coke.

Everywhere the fog grips the throat and sets the eyes watering. It puts out clammy fingers that touch the ears and give the hands a ghostly grip.

Children alone love it. They press their small faces to window-panes and watch the lights like little unripe oranges going by in the murk. A taxicab becomes something ogreish ; a steam-lorry is a dragon spitting flame and grunting on its evil way. Men who sell things in the streets become more than ever deliciously horrible and blood-curdling ; they never arrive normally ; they loom ; they appear, delightfully freezing the blood, howling their wares like the lonely wolf in a picture book.

I go out into the fog and enter an incredible underworld. The fog has turned London into a place of ghosts. At one moment a man with a red nose and a moustache like a small scrubbing-brush appears with the startling suddenness of an apparition. There must be millions of such men

34

with exactly similar moustaches, but this one is segregated from the herd. He seems unique in his isolation. I am quite prepared to believe he is the only one of that type in the world. I want to examine him as a learned man examines an insect on a pin. He seems a rare and interesting specimen. I want to cry "Stop! Let me appreciate you!" But no; in a flash he goes, fades—disappears!

There comes a girl, pale and beautiful—much more beautiful than she would be on a fine day, because the eyes are focussed on her alone! She has the allurement of a dream, or a girl in a poem.

What is this in Oxford Street? Two motor-cars locked together. Fifty grim, muffled ghosts stand round watching and blowing their noses. On any day but a foggy day it would be a mere nothing: an excuse for a policeman to lick his pencil and write in a book. To-day it is a struggle of pre-historic monsters in a death-grip. So must two clumsy, effete beasts of the Ice Age have fought locked in each other's scaly arms.

" Hi, there, put a bit of beef behind it. . . . Come on, mate—heave ! "

Deep, angry voices come from the grey nothing-ness. A girl ghost says :

" Oh, isn't it awful ? My eyes smart like anything."

Two big yellow eyes bear down on the scene. Men ghosts jump about in the road. They shout, they wave a red light, the monster with the two blazing eyes swerves, there is a vision of a red-faced man in a peaked cap and his gloved hands on a steering wheel :

" Keep your rear lights on, can't you ! You ought to be in the cemetery. . . . that's where you ought to be and that's where you'll blinkin' well end ! "

He passes on with his message.

* * *

In Finsbury Square a crowd of ghosts watch ten devils. Men are putting down asphalt. To-day they are not men : they are fiends pushing flaming cauldrons about. The roadway is a mass of tiny, licking, orange-coloured flames. The devils take long rakes, and the little flames leap and jump and fall over and between the prongs of the rakes like fluid. Red-hot wheeled trolleys, with a blasting flame, beneath them are dragged backwards and forwards over the roadway, heating it, licking at it, and roaring like furnaces.

The wind blows the flames this way and that way, lighting up the faces of the men, glittering on their belt buckles and making their bare arms fire colour.

The ghosts stand with white faces watching. More ghosts come. One little ghost has a peaked cap and an urgent message in a patent leather pouch. He stays a long time.

* * *

Near the Bank I come face to face with the greatest optimist of this or any other age. Here is a man entirely obscured by fog standing on the

Ghosts of the Fog

kerb making a tin monkey run up and down a piece of twine. Think of it! If you are sad or broke or things are going wrong, think of this man selling tin monkeys in a thick fog.

" How many have you sold ? " I ask him.

" Fower," he says.

Four tin monkeys sold in a thick fog.

Marvellous! Incredible!

Battle   *o*   *o*   *o*   *o*   *o*   *o*

THEY lie in long, bright wards, which are full of that clean hospital smell of warmth, flowers, and drugs. A neat-waisted nurse moves between the beds, smiling, bending, whispering, easing a pillow, passing from weary smile to weary smile, so young by contrast with these sufferers, so healthy, so calm, so reliable.

The women are mostly middle-aged, but their plaited hair, lying in two little coils over their shoulders, gives them a youthful look, so that you realize what they were like when they were eighteen. Some are pale, their poor, thin arms the colour of unbleached wax ; many look so well that you marvel that they should be there. It is the same in the men's wards. Cancer! That malignant, hissing word that lurks like a spectre at the back of so many minds has brought these men and women to one of the most noble hospitals in the world—the Free Cancer Hospital in the Fulham Road.

I admit that when I entered my first ward I shrank, in the shameful cowardice of my health, as I did once when a leper in the East rose up on his stumps out of the dust and touched my arm. To see the unimaginable horrors which you could be called on to suffer, to see lying there before your eyes the unthinkable depths to which your fine, strong body could sink, is a ghastly ordeal.

Yet what did I see ? I saw greater than this

black thing whose vileness no words can mitigate, the splendid forces of Heroism and Hope : Heroism in the long, quiet wards, Hope in the operating theatres, in the laboratories. Here in the middle of London, with streams of omnibuses thundering past beyond the railings, is a day and night battle with agony. Tragedy and triumph follow each other through these white halls, and over all is that fine spirit of enthusiasm as of an army banded to fight for a cause.

*   *   *

Instead of shuddering at the flesh, I reverenced the spirit that rises up and fights this unknown terror, fights it with the knife and with the test tube and with the X-ray, and goes on fighting, goes on hoping. Have you ever in a storm at sea thrilled to the driving, thrusting strength and balance of a great ship riding the tempest ? If so, you will know how I felt in this hospital that steers its course through an ocean of suffering.

" This is the laboratory ! "

A man in white overalls was bending over a microscope. Another man in white was examining the changing colour in a test tube. The rigid set of their shoulders denoted utter concentration. Round them lay hundreds of glass globes, bottles, ghastly exhibits from which I swiftly turned away.

Day in and day out, year after year, the research department of this hospital searches into the mysteries of cancer. In one part of the building doctors try to cure or alleviate the disease ; in another scientists work with their minds on that day when it may be possible to prevent it. Is there a more splendid room in London?

*   *   *

The chronic ward! Through glass doors I saw in one men, in another women. They were away from the other patients in whom the disease has been caught in time. I tried not to look at the seared faces; I turned from the broken lives with a soreness at my heart. Some of them have been there for years, some are there for life. Over many of them was a strange, still peace which made me see, but I may be wrong, a nurse hurrying down those calm corridors with a merciful hypodermic syringe in her hand.

*   *   *

Visiting day! Can you imagine the quiet heroism of it? The wife who comes to see the husband who has been taken away from her, the husband who creeps in towards a bed in which, so small and girlish and white, she lies waiting for him? The flowers, the little cheerfulnesses, and, behind it all, the doubt, the wondering, the ache, the sense of injustice.

"Well, you'll soon be well and home again, dear."

"Yes! And how's old Johnny? How I'd love to see that dog again!"

Then anxiously, swiftly in reply:

"But you *will*, you old silly, you *will*!"

"Yes, of course, perhaps I will."

"Good-bye!"

Battle

" Oh, come back, my dear.   Just once more !
How lovely your hair smells. . . ."

Can you imagine how often the most cheerful
visitor crumples up when the weary eyes from the
bed cannot see beyond the closed door ?

*   *   *

Who is Dr. William Marsden ?

How many Londoners know ?   He was the man
who seventy-one years ago founded this hospital,
and behind it lies a story as tragic as any in its
wards.   When going home late one night Dr.
Marsden, who was then a young medical student,
found a poor girl in a dying condition on a door-
step near Holborn.   He took her to a hospital,
where she was refused admission because she bore
no letter of introduction from a subscriber.   The
next day she died.   The young medical student
resolved that if he succeeded in life he would
found a free hospital for which there would be no
qualification for admission but poverty and
suffering.

He became famous, he loved, he married.   Then
his own wife was stricken with cancer, and nothing
could be done to check the disease.   Out of her
death and the death of the unknown woman
sprang this splendid work that shines like a good
deed over London.

Babies in the Sun   ᗧ   ᗧ   ᗧ   ᗧ

FAT babies, white dogs running, nursemaids
with the wind pulling at their snuff-coloured
veils, and at least six sharp intervals of sun strong
enough to paint three shadows on the grass. That
was how Kensington Gardens looked the other
day, that delicious annexe to a thousand nurseries,
that lovely land of young things insulated from
our common world by a row of spiked railings.

I went up the Broad Walk revelling in this
untroubled side of life, joyfully appreciating other
people's babies, patting other people's dogs,
admiring a smart turnout that lacked only a crest
on the dove-grey perambulator, noting with pleasure
the tall, neat young Kensington mothers with
their lamp-post figures in well-cut tweed. When
the sun came through it was like a game of musical
chairs. The nursemaids stopped perambulating.
Wind-blown walkers came to a standstill. They
sat down on green seats.

So did I.

Next to me was a maiden of about three, a
little unopened rose-bud of a girl, whose crisp gold
hair escaped from a woollen cap with a yellow
woollen tuft on top like a tangerine. Her short
legs, in grey woollen trousers, stuck out in space
so that she, sitting on a grown-up's seat, was in
exactly the same position she would have assumed
had she been sitting on a floor ! Her brother was
perhaps five. He wore a peaked cap of corduroy,

Babies in the Sun

leggings, and a little fawn coat with an absurd belt at the back.

These two were holding hands, a difficult feat, I imagine, when hands are so small and woollen gloves so bulky and fluffy. They were discussing railway travel. He said that the carriage wheels say " lickety-lick, lickety-lick," which I thought was very true, but she, womanlike, contradicted him, saying that they go " tell-at-a-train, tell-at-a-train," which I thought also was very true. Then suddenly he said loudly three times, because his nurse was reading a novel :

" Nannie," he said, " I'm going to marry Madge ! "

She looked shocked, put down the novel, and said :

" No, Master John, little boys don't marry their sisters, ever."

" I know," said Master John. " Not now, of course, but when I grow up and get big. Some day when I'm——"

Here he opened his arms to denote size and maturity.

" Yes ; but then you'll marry some other boy's sister," said the nurse.

" I won't—not never ! " cried John furiously. " I'll marry Madge ! Other boys' sisters are silly asses. They play with dolls ! "

The sun went in and they went away, nurse telling him that " nice boys " don't say " silly asses "—ever ! I smiled. Little minds in fairy-land grappling for the first time with this incomprehensible world ! Poor John, dear Madge !

The Heart of London

Ten minutes in the Broad Walk make you think a lot about small children. How much character they show at an age when they seem hardly to exist as reasonable beings! See how some lag behind, how others are unhappy unless they are in front, exploring, climbing, meeting great dogs on which, at the last moment, they turn their backs in fear. Watch how some just endure a walk placidly, while others shine with the adventure of it, seeing every detail, wondering, questioning. Look how some collect things busily: sticks by the armful, stones by the pocketful! Restless, acquisitive little creatures. All instinct with motives planted in them before birth.

How amusing it is to watch it all. Such tiny, instinctive people'

*　　　*　　　*

The Round Pond flecked by wind. White gulls. Ducks with green velvet heads. Not one ship slanting across this ocean; not one. Only a boy prodding the water with a stick:

"Too cold to sail a ship!" I said.

"It isn't," he replied, scowling. "But mother thinks it is."

"And she's right!" I said, wishing to rebuke him.

"She isn't!" (Slap, slap on the water.)

"She is!"

"She isn't!"

I felt that this conversation had all the elements of eternity, so, after delivering a last word in defence of the mothers of Kensington who release the navies of the Round Pond at exactly the right temperature, I left this scowling die-hard admiral to his melancholy.

*   *   *

Then, on a path under bare trees, I saw a fat, round fairy in salmon pink. Just standing, she was. I sat down to look at her. She advanced slowly. Among the bare trees someone called, " Joan, Joan ! " She reminded me of a faun I saw once on the Rock of the Loreli on the Rhine. It advanced in just this same doubtful, solemn manner ; one movement on my part would have sent it with beating heart into the thicket. So she advanced. I smiled ; she smiled. Then she touched my coat with one finger, laughed, and—ran unsteadily away over the path under bare trees. Flirt !

I left Wonderland, and caught an omnibus to Piccadilly in a remarkably good temper. . . .

Faces in the Strand ∽ ∽ ∽ ∽

WHEN you ride up the Strand on top of an omnibus—and probably in rain—please remember that someone is envying you with all his heart, that someone would give six months' pay to sit in your damp seat and see the lines of traffic converge on Charing Cross.

To the west in Canada, to the south in Africa, to the east in India, and far over the sea in Australia and New Zealand, are the lonely men. Where the red border line of Empire ends on the map in an alien colour are the little outposts in which these men work and dream. At the end of day they ram down the tobacco in their pipes and think of home with the characteristic sentimentality of the exile, for solitude makes a man very like a child. " Lord to be in London now ! " How many times in the twenty-four hours does this cry go up all over the earth ? We who take our London carelessly as a matter of course can have no conception of its meaning to these wanderers who, feeling the ache of home-sickness, are too old to cry.

* * *

The Strand !

That means London in shack, bungalow, and camp. It means more : it symbolizes—home ! Not Piccadilly, not Pall Mall, not fashionable Mayfair or Belgravia, but the curious old Victorian Strand.

What a street it is. It does not belong to

Faces in the Strand

London. Piccadilly, Regent Street, and Oxford Street stole its birthright long ago. It belongs to the Empire. Look at its shops. They are full of pith helmets and spine pads, veld shirts and tropical drill, ammunition belts and puttees. Your smart subaltern going out to join the Indian cavalry may buy his clothes in Savile Row, but your old colonial, who has been pegging down the flag somewhere for the best part of his life, comes back to shop in the Strand, to walk in the Strand, to exult in the Strand. . . .

* * *

Take the faces. In days when colonials come home you will find nothing more interesting in London. The exile makes straight for the Strand; if he does not know it he makes its acquaintance at once, joyfully, reverently; for he has heard men speak of it as men speak of their mothers. As he walks along he begins to believe that he has really come home.

You will see him shouldering his way gingerly through the crowds with the gentleness of a big man not used to pavements, and he looks up at the landmarks, a shop where he bought a gun once, a restaurant where once Mary . . . well, never mind, that was over long ago. Or he may be that strange thing, a tenderfoot in London, a tenderfoot from the prairies or the veld or the Afghan frontier. He is fulfilling his destiny: He is walking down the Strand! When he gets back men will say to him: " Well, and how did you find London ? "

The Heart of London

And he will start a story consciously and proudly with :

" I was walking down the Strand one morning——"

Ah, he has struck a chord at once. Surely you visualize the smile that will go round the circle of men deep in their cane chairs. " I was walking down the Strand ! " Can you begin a story in the tropics in a more arresting way ? You set a whole flock of memories a-flying. . . .

What sentimental journeys the Strand has seen. You must have been stopped at some time near the Adelphi by a burnt-up, middle-aged man who asks the way to a bar or a restaurant unknown to you. When you say you don't know it, a disappointed look creeps into his eyes, and he apologizes and goes off, very straight and lonely, in the crowd.

Conrad in quest of his youth ? Perhaps. Possibly for years, while he waited for leave, he was promising himself a visit to this place. No doubt the stars saw him sitting out alone at night thinking of it, hearing the thunder of the Strand, seeing its lights, and himself slipping into his old seat at a corner table where he used to sit with old X, who was killed in " British East." . . .

All the time the Strand was altering, denying such exiles their beloved landmarks.

*   *   *

So they drift a little sadly and disconsolately along the Strand, feeling as you feel when, after a long absence, you visit a place known to you when

Faces in the Strand

you were a child.   Nothing is so big as you thought,
nothing so impressive as once it was.   That tiny
paddock was once a prairie—that small house a
castle.

The Strand to them is somehow different—
cheaper, smaller, vaguely disappointing.   Those
pale-faced men hurrying along.   How strange.
What an altered atmosphere !   And where are
those lovely little faces that used to look from
beneath Merry Widow hats ?

*   *   *

Then, six months after, in a solitude of stars
and palms, with a hot wind blowing over the plains :
" O Lord, to see the dear old Strand now ! "
The big stars shine, the moon swings up above
the distant hills, and the old love comes back
into the heart of the lonely man. . . .

Women and Tea ✏ ✏ ✏ ✏

A TEA-SHOP is a delightful place. It is the milestone that marks the end of a day's work.

In the provinces, and particularly in the north and in Scotland, where men take tea with passionate sincerity, frequently starting with sardines and ending with apple tart, the tea-shop occupies an appropriately massive position in daily life. London's tea-shops are, however, talk-shops, refuges from a day's shopping, trysting-places after a terrible eight hours' separation.

O, the eyes that meet over a muffin every afternoon in London ; the hands that thrill to a casual touch beneath the crumpet plate. . . .

London's tea-shops are of many kinds, from the standardized shop to the good pull-up for millionaires constructed on the Paris plan, where slim Gruyère sandwiches hide in paper coats, and cakes taste of Benedictine, and bills have a queer habit of working out at fifteen shillings.

Then, of course, there is the cosy type of tea-shop run on amateur lines where genteel young women who do not seem to have forgotten William Morris bend wistfully over the meringues in brown or sage green *crêpe de Chine* gowns and an air of shattered romance. Such places have fanciful names designed to attract those with a passion for peace. They are always opening or going smash, and there is a widespread belief in the

Women and Tea

suburbs among enterprising young women that this is the way to an enormous bank account.

" Thanks awfully ! "

That's what they say when you pay the bill, and such a sad, sweet smile goes with it. Andromeda chained to a cheese cake.

*   *   *

I entered a large musical tea-shop in the heart of Shopland yesterday. The atmosphere was as feminine as that of a perfume store. It was No Man's Land. I steered my conspicuous way to a table through a jungle of musquash, moleskin, and beaver. The only other men there were in the toils of women, politely tapping their *éclairs*, and wearing photographic faces, behaving as men never behave away from this uplifting and ennobling atmosphere.

I heard a girl describe a bridesmaid's dress ; another girl was talking about a baby ; a third had discovered John Galsworthy. Two young married women were discussing their husbands, how really sweet they were, how they hated cold mutton, how amusingly irritable they were, and how upset they were when their wives shingled their hair. . . .

A slight stir was caused by the entrance of husbands to claim their wives. One, a handsome young man, was charmingly introduced with shy pride ; another, an elderly, bluff, old-established husband, was received quite calmly like an over-due muffin. Then the human event that electrified the entire tea-shop happened, that marvellous touch of nature that unites Kennington with even the best parts of Kensington.

A small, smug child, distinguished only by a red balloon on the end of a string, set up a wild and awful howl. It was dramatic in its suddenness. Everybody looked round in the belief that the infant had sat on a pin. Instead they saw the red balloon drifting with a gay and careless determination towards the roof. Reaching its destination, it bumped gracefully twice and remained there, coyly nestling against a frescoed cupid.

Immediately the entire tea-shop, hitherto split into self-centred groups, became one in a solid endeavour to rescue the red balloon. Young men anxious to distinguish themselves stood on chairs and made wild grabs for the string with their umbrellas ; dogs which till then had been asleep and unsuspected, awakened and barked.

In the centre of the stage stood the smug, small child, breathless with anxiety, pointing to the roof, grief-stricken that his balloon had played him false, yet encouraged by the stir the event was causing in so many grown-up lives.

A grim old man melted by the tragedy obtained a long pole employed in pulling down shop blinds. He succeeded in driving the balloon from its fastness and sending it fatuously bumping into another. Meanwhile the entire shop held its breath, expecting these good intentions to end in a loud plop and a worse tragedy. There was a gasp of relief as this ancient hero gave way to a man in an apron with a step-ladder.

Women and Tea

He did the deed.

The tea-shop settled down. The smug child that had united an afternoon's assembly left unnoticed. Over the tea-tables rose again the talk of bridesmaids and husbands and shingles and Maud's hennaed hair. The orchestra played some more Puccini, and a small boy who had profited by the commotion to seize his fourth *éclair* gave an enormous sigh of joy.

An Open Door ✺ ✺ ✺   ✺   ✺

SHORTLY after midnight a decently dressed young man glanced furtively round Trafalgar Square, hesitated a moment, and then ran swiftly up the broad, black steps of St. Martin's Church. I came up behind him as he tapped the door.

There was the sound of a drawn bolt, and the door swung back. The young man stammered. He was blue with cold, and—there was something else :

" I'm—I'm broke," he said. " I've never done this before. I've always had a bit of money ; but —well, I've nowhere to sleep to-night, and—please can I come in ? "

The door opened wider, and a pleasant, middle-aged policewoman said :

" Come along ! " I followed.

*   *   *

Down in the crypt of St. Martin's Church, the church whose doors never close, I saw a remarkable sight. Broad, white arches spanned a dim gloom. Certain benches were set facing the east, as in the church above, and others were placed round the crypt. Lying, sitting upright, and huddled in every position of which the human body is capable, were men and women, homeless wanderers over the hard face of the earth.

There was no sound in the white crypt but

54

variously keyed snores and the small scratch of a policewoman's pen as she kept a record of Christ's guests, for such they are ; and as I looked at them these words sang in my heart : " Come unto Me, all ye that labour and are heavy laden, and I will give you rest."

Sanctuary. That was it. They had the hunted air of having run hard to find this place, and, having found it, had abandoned themselves to safety. There was something else. They reminded me of a picture that used to thrill me when I was a child : troops, rolled in their cloaks beside dead fires, sleeping before a battle. Their battle was To-morrow.

*   *   *

There was a young girl who could not sleep. She was wrapped tightly in a blue mackintosh. She sat with her eyes wide open, gazing before her. There was a grey-haired woman sleeping upright in a pew, a poor, rakish hat on a pile of prayer-books beside her. Three or four other women slept near together, leaning against each other, as if for warmth.

Most of the men slept. Some had no overcoats, and lay huddled with their tousled heads on hassocks. Others had placed their coats over their heads. One or two wore spats, and appeared from their clothes to be prosperous. Then you looked at their boots, and read a story of tramp, tramp, tramp. One elderly man, awakened suddenly, shot out an arm to look at his wrist-watch. But there was no watch there, and he drew his hand swiftly under his coat again as though it hurt.

*   *   *

" Some extraordinary dramas have been acted on the steps outside in the small hours," said a young man officially connected with the church. " Once a girl was saved from white-slavers ; once I brought in a boy so blue with cold that I had to open the furnace doors without delay, and thaw him. Most of the ' down-and-outs ' know this church. Many of them we manage to set up again, some sink back or just disappear. Yet we never lose faith in human nature. A homeless person is allowed to shelter here only three nights in succession. After that we try to find some other abode, so you see our visitors are always changing."

He opened a door, and I found myself in a cellar full of old clothes. Boxes of collars lay on the floor. A knowing looking silk hat crowned a pile of old hats. Women's skirts and men's trousers hung from pegs. Boots and shoes stood neatly dressed by the right.

" This is our wardrobe," he said. " Our first principle is to give a homeless person food and then whatever clothes we can. You can't expect to hear the truth on an empty stomach."

" Are you often deceived by people who drift in here out of the night ? "

" Now and then. It's nothing compared with the friends we make, the delightful characters we discover when the ache and pain of hardship have

worn off. We divide men into three groups :
Those who have been to prison and have a grudge
against the world ; those who went to the war as
boys and came back men with boys' minds ; and
those who simply will not work and can't run
straight. We have heard every fairy tale in the
world, and we know a scrounger at sight ! "

*　　*　　*

I tip-toed back through the white crypt. The
pale girl was still awake. The grey-haired woman
still slept—old, worn-out, uncared-for, and life
gone by. Men slept and stirred uneasily as if
afraid of the dawn that was stealing on to draw
them again into the battle. How many would
rise gloriously ; how many fall ? We talk of
human nature in the rough, heartbeats, life. Here
it is in the middle of London every night, each
sleeper a real drama of struggle, each man and
woman midway in that Valley of the Shadow
through which all lives, spiritually or materially,
must pass.

"We don't care what they are," said the young
man. "If they are in trouble, that is enough."

I hardly heard him, for I was thinking that in
this white place is the Spirit of Christ.

A Bit of Bagdad   *o*   *o*   *o*   *o*

THE only place where you could sell an elephant, a were-wolf, or your second best aunt without attracting the slightest curiosity is Club Row, a Sunday market famous throughout the eastern regions of London. Turn out of Shoreditch along the Bethnal Green Road and presently you see a large cloth-capped crowd. You approach.

A dramatic, sinister man who lost his razor early last year detaches himself and sidles up to you with his right hand suspiciously hidden in the breast of his coat. Is he an anarchist? Just as you expect him to bring out a bomb and cry "Down with Civilization," he quickly produces a six-ounce pom and whispers in a voice like a rusty door hinge : "Come on, half a dollar!" Other dog men approach. They offer handfuls of pups, or they submit dogs of larger growth which sit round in a circle looking up at you questioningly, hopefully. You want to buy the lot. Then an Airedale bites a collie and you find yourself the centre of a splendid battle, from which you escape into the heart of the mob.

Here life is magnificent. Thousands of things are happening at once in Oriental variety. This is what Bagdad was like in the days of the Caliph. This is what the Mouski in Cairo is like to-day. As you stand wedged between people who hold sacks that writhe and cluck, a man waves a couple of buff orpingtons in your face and pushes past to stand himself a glass of jellied eels. An elderly parrot-like old lady is marooned helplessly, with a green aloof-looking parrot, exactly like herself, perched on her hand. Pigeons coo, hens cackle, cockerels crow, dogs bark, canaries sing, and you gain the impression that anything—anything—is yours for " half a dollar."

I was interested in the little groups round contortionists, catch-penny men, and herb doctors. We have driven these mediæval characters from more polite places, and it is almost with a thrill that east of Aldgate Pump you find yourself in the hearty atmosphere of a fair as old as England. One man, who said that his face was as well known as the dome of St. Paul's, walked rapidly up and down with a mysterious paper packet over which he held a pair of dental forceps. Every one wanted to see what marvellous thing he would pick out of the packet at the psychological moment. All the time as he walked backwards and forwards he talked of indigestion and other things with Elizabethan frankness. He discussed food as if it were a revolver.

" If the steak repeats, if the onions repeat, if the pudding repeats, if cheese repeats. . . ."

Then, working up to his climax, he dived the forceps into the packet and produced a beautiful heliotrope-coloured pill !

Did he sell any ? He did !

Under a railway arch a young man with a faint Scottish accent had been handcuffed and chained. Round his neck he wore a steel collar ; on his head a steel cap which, he said, was " an exact replica of the cap used for capital punishment throughout the United States of America." (Thrill in the audience !)

" And now," he remarked (with a touch of his Scottish accent), " before I release myself, my partner will take the liberty of passing the hat round ! "

The fringes of the crowd melted away. After a prolonged struggle, interrupted by a donkey and cart bursting violently into the arena, the young man unshackled himself, dived for the hat, looked at the pennies, and remarked, " Well, now ; if any sportsman would care. . . ."

But the crowd had stampeded.

How delightfully childish it all is. In order to sell chocolate one man had taken off his coat and had put on his head an irresponsible looking opera hat !

In side streets I came on a bicycle market. I wondered how many were doped like racehorses. A stray bicycle found carelessly outside a house becomes something quite different with the aid of a paint pot ! How many old crocks had been dressed up with new lamps and saddles I would not care to say ! Here trade was booming. I saw a man who had bought a dog, a birdcage, and a pair of pink braces, treat himself to a pair of handle-bars. It must be wonderful to wander through Bagdad like this, meeting things on the way, living an hour full of infinite possibilities, not knowing whether you will arrive home with a bullfinch or a bicycle ! After watching this market

A Bit of Bagdad

closely I realize this : people do not go there to buy things, but to have things sold to them !

*   *   *

On the way out I saw something worth while. A melancholy bull pup sitting in the road with all the world's troubles in his eyes was picked up by a little girl.

" I want him because he looks so unhappy."

A chauffeur in a green coat paid out five shillings.

" Darling . . . darling," said the girl, holding the squat little body.

They took him to a motor-car that had been left round the corner. So he left a street corner in Bagdad to be a prince among pups.

Kismet !

"Prisoners Only" ⚬ ⚬ ⚬ ⚬

"PRISONERS Only."

A door in Bow Street Police Station opens on a small tiled room in which each morning all the prisoners on their way to the celebrated dock gather to await the call.

It is an exclusive apartment. Visitors are not allowed. Unless you break a shop window, punch a policeman in the stomach, or become publicly full of spirit you will never see it. It was due only to the courtesy of Bow Street that I was allowed in for a moment yesterday like an ordinary prisoner. Here I found a strange assortment of human beings gathered together by Fate—or should I say alcohol?—for Monday morning's crime originates in a bottle!

The room is tiled and looks like an ordinary waiting-room till a policeman opens the door that leads out to a courtyard and then you see a second door composed of stout iron bars. About twenty or thirty men were sitting round the room talking to the policemen who had arrested them. Most of them were weary, some of those who had been let out on bail looked smart, a few still retained traces of their fateful debauch, and all had lost the divine afflatus which had flung them into a pair of blue arms. The atmosphere was rather like that of a headmaster's study in which is gathered a group of bad boys waiting for the cane.

A stoical old man dozed peacefully in a corner.

" Prisoners Only "

So might dear old Falstaff have bared his grey
hairs in a moment of regrettable trial. A navvy
with the head of a Roman emperor sat huddled
in his clay-soiled clothes, silent, grim. He
reminded me of Trajan's bust in the British
Museum. He should have been dressed in a toga
instead of sitting in Bow Street with a fine of five
shillings hanging over him! A young man with
a mild face sat near him, the kind of young man
who keeps rabbits in a back yard. I wondered
what odd circumstance had brought him in conflict with law and order. Among a group of seedy
and tattered people I noticed a smart man wearing
spats and holding a neat umbrella.

It was the strangest roomful you can imagine.

*   *   *

How wonderfully British! I do not imagine
that the police and prisoners of any other nation
meet together as captor and captive in the same
cheery, almost social atmosphere.

In Berlin I imagine it must be exceedingly
unpleasant to be a prisoner, and in Paris, also, it
cannot be exactly jolly. In Cologne I once saw
a German policeman draw his sword and charge
a little boy who had left a banana skin on a patch
of neat, cultured turf ; and in Paris once I saw a
gendarme do unnecessarily unfriendly things to
his captive. But our Roberts are not like this,
and when they are face to face with their prey in
the station they seem almost apologetic about it :

" You broke the law and I did my duty, and
that's that. Let's forget it ! "

That is the atmosphere in the " Prisoners Only "
room. Thumbs in belts, the policemen talked
with their prisoners about racing, the weather,
and, as far as I could gather, anything but drink
and brawls. What instinctive good breeding!
Here and there a prisoner who took his captivity
lightly laughed and joked with the man who
brought him there.

" What'll I get ? " one prisoner asked.

" Oh, about twenty years without option ! "
replied the constable. Then a man with a note-
book became busy with the day's evil-doers, a
name was called, and as the first prisoner pulled
himself together and strode out dockwards, a flutter
of interest went round the waiting-room, and the
old man awakened with a start and asked where
he was.

*   *   *

Under the Royal Arms sat Sir Chartres Biron,
white-haired and exceedingly wise to human
nature. He was dealing with a pathetic collection
of women prisoners who had been waiting in a
" Prisoners Only " room of their own. Constable
after constable described scenes of revelry in which
it was alleged that certain inadequate Bacchantes
in black bonnets had been urged to deeds of violence.

Some women pleaded guilty and got it all over
quickly. Others clasped and unclasped their
hands—appealing, thin, worn hands grimed with
work—and tried to impress Sir Chartres that
" two glasses of port " had been the cause of all
their trouble. They were fined and went their
way, some with an assumption of belated dignity,

others jauntily. One old lady was so pleased with
her sentence that she danced down the corridor
between two lines of policemen promising never
to look upon the wine again.

*   *   *

Then one by one my friends of the waiting-room
came up for justice : drunk and disorderly, drunk
in charge of a motor-car, creating a disturbance,
using insulting language. They all looked sorry
for themselves and exceedingly foolish. Five deaf
and dumb youths had, it appeared, pushed a
policeman off the pavement. The mother of one
of them interpreted the case, talked to them in
baby language, asked them if they had really
" banged " the policeman. They nodded their
heads and tried to speak, but only vague, tortured
sounds, heart-rending to hear, came from their
mouths. They filed out, bound over.

Then Cæsar strode into the dock, said he had
been drunk, accepted his fine without a trace of
emotion, and walked from the dock with an
invisible cohort before him and—a visible bottle
sticking out of his coat-tails !

*   *   *

When he has done his day's work does Sir
Chartres Biron feel more like laughing or crying,
I wonder ?

65

Boys on the Bridge ✺ ✺ ✺ ✺

BOYS are always leaning over London
Bridge, as right-minded boys have been
leaning these five hundred years and more.
Beneath them the Thames, that loved river of
ours, swirls and eddies round the piers, sucking at
the weathered stone as it runs seawards, out and
away.

When I joined them the other day I noticed
with an authentic thrill that against the grim
wharves men were doing interesting things in
ships. No matter how trivial the act—the hauling
of a rope, the turning of a winch, the painting of a
hull—it becomes somehow vital and significant to
anyone on dry land. To a London office boy who
has been told not to linger by the wayside—ah !
how exquisite, how irresistible !

Sometimes little important jets of steam rose
from a cargo boat, marvellously suggesting departure and the imminence of great adventure ;
enviable free men whose boots had never trod
an office stair popped their heads out of hatchways
and lumbered up on deck ; a string of linked
barges, dingy, low in the water, went by behind
an impertinent tug, which nosed the tide sideways,
pulling and puffing. On the hindmost barge a
man was frying bacon in a jet-black pan. O,
exquisite ! O, irresistible ! Was this not life ?
Was this not romance ?

To me a fat white woman was singularly signifi-

Boys on the Bridge

cant. She appeared from the bowels of a barge and, moving slowly to starboard with a nautical roll, hung an intimate item of her laundry right in the eye of London Bridge. Then she looked round her with that composed placidity which sustains the suburbs (just as if she were in Brixton and not on the high seas), and after giving one of her sleeves a roll to keep it above her fat elbow, she went below with the important air of the busy female who believes that her industry is the hinge on which life turns smoothly. No cut-throats on that barge, no swashbuckling, no silly ideas about the Spanish Main there, but everything nice and tidy, and wipe your boots on the mat and mind you don't stay out too long after closing time! Wonderful how a woman—any woman—softens a masculine scene and awakens the boy in man to a swift respect—as if the matron had appeared suddenly on the scene of a scrum on a dormitory landing! The wild places of the earth do not care much about a man. He can't do much! When the woman appears the aspens shiver and the tamarisks tremble and even the oak is fearful, for a lone man is transitory and woman is permanent : she means a home and a whole lot more men ; she is the beginning of civilization.

So the fat woman made her barge most interesting to me : she brought it right into society, she humanized the wild old Thames. All this was high above the office boys who pressed their stomachs to the stone and clambered for a foothold in the balustrading so that they might take a better view of all this glamour. . . .

The Heart of London

Thames, you muddy strip of magic, how many London heads have you turned ; how many sirens come in from sea on every tide to sing those wicked songs against which we poor chained creatures sometimes wax our ears in vain ?

*   *   *

I looked at the faces of the spellbound office boys. They gazed like gargoyles from the parapet. Most of them were dull and stolid ; but you never can tell ! Their cheeks bulged with sweets and their eyes regarded the river with the same intent vacancy that they would have given to a spectacular road repair.

One face only seemed to me to hold the hunger that burns. It belonged to a thin, pale lad who possessed no physical strength, the type that would rather have been Hercules than Homer ; the frail type that dreams of swords and ambuscades and blood. He looked out over the water towards Tower Bridge with eyes that were wide—whether with imagination or indigestion I cannot say ! I can only tell you this : he was the kind of pale, useless mass of parental despair that through history has met the turning point of existence in an idle hour, when imagination, blazing suddenly like fired straw, illuminates a dream on which to build a life.

What was he thinking, I wondered. Had I asked him he would have said sullenly, " Nothing," and have slouched away, ashamed.

I wondered if he was seeing in Thames water those things that thousands of London boys have seen—argosies and ventures and foreign places, the drive of water past a vessel's bows, leaning sails, and small white towns whose palm trees stand with their feet in calm lagoons.

Who knows? This is the dream of London Bridge. This is the challenge that the Thames flings down to London every day and every night, crying it aloud to the huddled streets and to the crowded places, calling it softly in the market-place. This is the old magic. It has given to London merchants, adventurers, sailors, poets, and millions of poor, discontented men who must need take their burning hearts to Balham and shut their ears.

* * *

Slowly conscience dawned in the minds of the boys. One by one they went away, their places immediately filled by others.

Away they went into the traffic, to become lost in the ant-hills of commerce, carrying who knows what high resolve from that stolen moment beside the river.

* * *

More barges came downstream slowly. High and shrill sounded the hoarse protest of a siren, imperative and wild, and I seemed to feel, right in the heart of London, where all things are so ordered and inevitable, the ancient call to the open places that comes with the smell of tar and the sight of thin masts rising to the sky.

Night Birds ∘ ∘ ∘ ∘ ∘

IT is three o'clock in the morning. Piccadilly Circus is empty of life and movement—save for a prowling policeman trying shop doors, and a group of men directing water from a giant hose over the gleaming, empty road.

A taxicab is an event, and a stray person walking quietly into the Circus holds dramatic possibilities. The mind fastens on him. Who is he ? He may be a great criminal, or a great lover walking home after a dance with his head full of glorious dreams, or he may be a burglar, or a young man who has just inherited a million, or a young man without a place to rest his head. The emptiness of Piccadilly at three a.m. is awful, unnatural, death-like. . . .

Yet London is not asleep. Hundreds of people in London never seem to sleep. Come into one of the all-night cafés which have sprung up within the last year or so. It is full. It hums with talk and laughter. Waiters move about between the crowded tables. There is a constant clatter of cups and saucers, and the air is blue with smoke. In contrast with the desolation of the empty streets outside, it is an astonishing place. At first you think there is nothing to distinguish the café from the same place at normal hours. You look again and realize the difference. The people are different. The woman with three or four brown paper parcels—the shopping woman—is

Night Birds

absent. There are no children. Few elderly
people.

Those present are mostly young people distinguished either by an air of lassitude or an
unnatural hectic gaiety.

At the next table a girl is eating lobster salad.
Lobster at three a.m. !

*　　*　　*

Who are these people ? You begin to wonder
about them. Some are obvious—extremely obvious—some are mysteries.

In a corner a man in evening dress has dropped
in for a cup of coffee with the nice girl with whom
he has been dancing. She keeps her velvet
evening cloak tightly round her, and looks about
at the other people, trying to fix them. It is to
her an adventure. Her partner's glance at her
over the broad rim of his cup suggests that he is
desperately trying to prolong the " night out."
He is a clean, blonde young man, and he pretends
to take no notice of the elderly satyr at another
table who is openly admiring the girl in the cloak.
But she sees and gives the satyr a cold Kensington
eye, hard as an eviction order.

Quite a number of other dancers seem glued to
rolls and coffee, unable to go home. They laugh
and discuss the dance. Someone says : " I must
be in the office at nine ! " They laugh and order
more coffee.

A group of men with music cases under the
chairs talk in a corner. They are a jazz band
which has just finished work. There are a number

of solemn, self-centred men smoking quietly, alone. They may be night-workers, post office officials, or what not, waiting for the next tramcar.

There are inevitable Japanese students. They sit together talking, occasionally taking an expressionless survey of the company. What are they doing ? Studying night life ? Winding up an innocent party ?

Most interesting are the unplaceable people : the number of foreign-looking young men who argue together : the type of man who at the precise crack of Doom with graves opening and the world closing, would try to sell you a cheap pearl tiepin. A number of night birds are evidently in the habit of drinking coffee at three a.m. There is movement from table to table, group to group. Dotted about the room are girls who would describe themselves as dance instructresses or cinema actresses.

Four or five men who look as though they have been celebrating a friend's last night of bachelor-hood enter with exaggerated politeness, apologizing for occasional conflicts with chairs and tables. They order black coffee. Another man comes up to their table. They all leap up and shake hands. " The last time I saw you was in Bagdad ! " he says. " What's happened to old ' Whisky Willie ' of the Gunners ? You remember that night. . . ."

This sort of talk still goes on in London where young men are linked together by common memories of the War.

*　　*　　*

Night Birds

As we go from the brilliantly lit room the
emptiness and the chill of sleeping London meets
us at the door. Long lines of lights shining on
desolate pavements, a shuffling figure under a
lamp, a slow taxicab cruising near the kerb, and
then, surprisingly, like a ghost of old London, a
hansom cab standing in Piccadilly, the ancient
horse, head down as if remembering past things!

In the cold air is the vague promise of a new
day, a faint rumble of market carts and vans as
if London stirs in her impressive slumber.

At the Wheel ∘ ∘ ∘ ∘ ∘

HE was sitting in the acrid unpleasantness of a London fog holding a steering-wheel and—the lives of men and women. It was Sunday.

Inside the well-lit and almost pleasant omnibus a young man, wearing his Sunday hat, and a young girl, completely Sundayfied, sat holding hands as they pretended to read a newspaper. They saw no more than each other's eyes, and what more could they possibly have seen ? Portentous women with unnaturally clean children entered or made a fussy exit from time to time, bent, no doubt, on that awfulness of a London Sunday—a visit to relatives. On some faces you could read a kind of comfortable condescension that somehow suggested a glittering descent on poor relations ; on others a dutiful resignation— the composure of an ordained martyr preparing to meet the lions—and you pictured a stiff and patronizing tea in a distant but exalted suburb, with criticism underlying an afternoon of smooth insincerity !

All the time the Man at the Wheel exhibited a broad and stocky back to the human comedy he was carrying ; sometimes his face, tense and questioning, was turned towards the lit interior as he tried to gauge the right moment to accelerate after the descent of an agile passenger. Mostly, however, he just sat there peering into the white

At the Wheel

cotton-wool world of fog that was hung with saffron lights, his big hands in gloves, expertly and suddenly taking his vehicle from an unexpected near rush of light as a tramcar clanged past. And the passengers did not notice him. They had paid twopence to be taken in safety through the fog!

*   *   *

I sat there frankly admiring him.

I have never heard of any poet writing an ode to a London omnibus driver, but he always strikes me as worthy subject of praise. He may not possess the social charm of the old horse-omnibus driver, who, according to legend, wore a top hat and used his whip butt on London as a lecturer uses a wand. He is a more solemn character. Machines always leave their mark on men. The big petrol engine has created a grim, silent, crouching character who, fortunately for London and Londoner's wives and families, has no time for social pleasantries as he urges his great, red, double-decked steed through the thousand perils of a crowded street.

He has, I think, developed a sixth sense. His whole being seems acutely conscious of inches. Watch the way a press of omnibuses in High Holborn or Tottenham Court Road, or any other famous hold-up, will edge and nudge a way with a mere inch between their mudguards, all so skilfully and calmly done as though the scarlet sides of the vehicles had nerves—invisible feelers —that carried warning of danger to the rough, deft hands at the wheel.

The Heart of London

As we crawled through the fog I watched his taut concentration, admired his judgment as he executed a circling movement round a candidate for suicide, as he jammed on the brakes within a yard of a halted motor-car, as he put on speed over a thin patch of fog, and as he shot ahead past a less speedy driver.

Now and then he had to crawl through a whiteness as dense as that terrible billowing mist that rolls down a Scottish mountain. Here and there pin-points of fire shone out, changed swiftly on approach into objects like long hair aflame in the wind, and, nearer still, stood revealed as tall fog flares shooting up in fire from metal standards.

At the terminus I watched the drivers dismount, stiff and cold, pull off their big gloves, and hit their cold hands across their chests. Wet particles of fog shone on their moustaches.

Pretty bad at Camden Town, and Baker Street was like a tunnel! Couldn't see a yard at Brixton. Fine and clear at the Crystal Palace. . . . So these adventurers of the London fog compared notes before, groping in remote recesses, they found money to buy coffee from a stall. Then a whistle, the roar of a chilled engine, and off again on their perilous pilgrimages across London.

Surely every man who has driven through fog with eyes that ache and imagine phantoms at each cross-road will be glad to raise his hat to the bulky figure behind the wheel of a London omnibus as he steers his living cargo to safety with no thought of praise because—it's all in the day's work?

Under the Dome   ◦   ◦   ◦   ◦

I WAS cheered to find that St. Paul's looked quite firm and permanent when I walked up Ludgate Hill the other morning. How deceptive are the works of man ! Who would have guessed that this mountain was feeling its age a bit, moving ever so slightly under the weight of its Dome ?

The pigeons wheeled in flight. A girl stood covered in them, while less bold birds walked, nodding quickly, round her feet pecking crumbs. Up the fine, bold sweep of the steps walked many people. I think that they were perhaps Londoners paying their first visit, hoping that they would get it over before the cathedral collapsed, for they looked up warily as they advanced as though alarmed by accounts of splitting piers, and then, finding nothing unusual, they went on their way, maybe surprised to find no cant to the Dome or any visible fissure !

As I walked over the black and white diamonds of the nave I realized that although I have attended services normal and national in St. Paul's I had never climbed to the Whispering Gallery. When Americans had talked to me about it I had lied and had pretended that I knew it. So I determined to wipe out my shame.

I walked down the south aisle admiring the gold shafts of light striking through the dusk of the church, noting the number of young women who

The Heart of London

go there to sit quietly and read sacred and profane literature, and remarking how one appreciative beam of light had caught a splendid head of Burne-Jones's hair, making it blaze in the comparative darkness like fire in a lovely thorn bush. I met all kinds of people wandering on tiptoe with that vague, lost air people assume in churches ; and then I came to a little office near the south transept in which I paid sixpence for a ticket— the best sixpennyworth, as I afterwards found, in all London.

" I thought," I said to the verger, " that I'd better go up there before it comes down here."

" That won't be for a long time, sir," he said with a reassuring smile, a sentiment I passed on at step two hundred and forty-one to a charming old lady, who asked if I thought it was " quite wise " to go right to the top !

What a climb it is ! If ever I go foolishly walking or climbing in Switzerland again I will get into training on this spiral staircase. Once up and once down every day and no mountaineer's muscles would be firmer, no walker's wind less treacherous. It is a fine, free, and uncrowded gymnasium !

Half-way up is a museum and a library, where I, puffing slightly, prodded about among old stones, the ruins of Old St. Paul's. I know no greater thrill than sightseeing. Then up, up, up and round and round again till I came to a little door at which a quiet, churchy man said it was the Whispering Gallery and told me to walk right round it.

Under the Dome

In the Whispering Gallery I was not so impressed by the man in occupation as I was by the astonishing bird's-eye view of tiny people walking far below on a little chess-board of a pavement. Then suddenly I heard a whisper. I looked across to the other side of the gallery. The guide was whispering against the wall. His message came to me like a spirit voice from the Beyond, rather terrifying and sepulchral: "The diameter of the dome is a hundred and eight feet," said the Voice, and then it plunged into an account of Sir Christopher Wren. I walked away, congratulated the Voice, which seemed gratified, and said, "How dissatisfied and hard of hearing some people are!"

High up below the dome of St. Paul's you have thrills. As you walk out on a large stone platform London lies below in a huddle of buildings and smoking chimneys. You pick out landmarks. How narrow even the widest streets look. To the east over the big black bulk of Cannon Street is the faint outline of Tower Bridge in the mist. Only the broad Thames has size. Men are midgets, an omnibus is blotted out from time to time by the flight of three pigeons; your eye rakes offices, exploring all floors at a glance, floors packed with typists. You feel like a beemaster looking into a hive; and all the time a rumble reaches you, the restless voice of the city.

*　　*　　*

Almost as wonderful as the smoky map of London spread below is the feeling that you, so

The Heart of London

leisurely examining St. Paul's while the rest of London is rushing about trying to pay the rent, are having a holiday in a foreign city.

You feel a superiority over all those poor harassed people. You perceive a new angle to London life. You join the idle drifting population of sightseers and you feel rather sorry you did not bring your camera with you, just to help out the illusion that you are in a Florentine mood.

Vergers, too, observe towards you the courtesy extended to strangers within the gate. There is a subtle difference in their manner. In their " Yes, sirs," and " No, sirs," and in their pointing and smiling you can feel the affection which churches have always, and quite rightly, extended to pilgrims. One man obviously considered me a distinguished visitor from foreign parts. He went out of his way to instruct me in history that I know quite well, and I wondered whether the only straight and honourable thing to do was to make a clean breast of it and stop him with :

" Look here, I live in Knightsbridge and work in Fleet Street, and I'm frightfully sorry about it, and all that. I know it's most unusual and you won't believe me, but there it is."

I had not the courage. I gazed insincerely into his enthusiastic eyes and said " Really ! " and " By Jove ! " and " How interesting," at appropriate pauses, so that when eventually I left him I went surrounded, for him, with all the beauty of a bird of passage.

Heartbreak House   *o*   *o*   *o*   *o*

IN the old comic papers you will find a stock
character whose nose is red, whose coat collar
is Astrakhan, whose hand is always drawn in the
act of conveying drink to a clean-shaven, mobile
mouth—a mouth always uttering the words :
" When I played Hamlet, laddie, in '84 . . . ."

He is, or rather was, the out-of-work actor.
No actor has of course ever been out of work :
he " rests " sometimes for so long a period that
idleness becomes a habit. Lack of employment
seems to cover the actor with disgrace. In most
other professions men make no secret of being
out of a job, but the actor acts both on and off
the stage.

The out-of-work actor to-day (you find him in
Leicester Square and the Charing Cross Road),
has changed since the comic papers pictured a
tragedian whose ambitious argosies had evidently
foundered in, as Homer would put it, a wine-dark
sea. To-day you find him in a bar, merely because
there he will meet other actors and agents and pick
up news of his heartless and overrated profession ;
but in his hand is a glass of ginger beer. His
clothes are well-cut and he wears a public school
tie. His spats draw attention to his worn boots,
always the sign of a man's condition, and as he
drawls lazily in his Oxford voice, real or assumed,
he tries hard to give the impression that, resting
as he is on the enormous profits of his genius, he

The Heart of London

must keep an important appointment in Mayfair at one-thirty or the duchess will be absolutely furious!

Poor brave people! No matter how overdue the rent may be they never lose their *panache*. To-day the fight to walk on in a musical comedy and say heartily: "Girls, let's go to Paris!" and the feminine fight to answer coyly in good Kensingtonian: "Oh, what a quate topping ideah!" is fiercer than ever. Added to the usual legitimate "resters" are thousands of film actors, both male and female, thrown on the streets because the British film trade is in the doldrums.

If you could only know the bitterness of the fight for the job that does not exist, the daily march round the agents' offices, the young man who puts his head round a door, smiles, says "Nothing doing"—the humiliation of not having a shilling!

What keeps them going? What encourages girls to wash their one pair of real silk stockings overnight, brush their furs carefully, and turn out each day, apparently prosperous, to try another joust with fate? It is belief in themselves, the inability to do anything else, and, above all, it is a vision of fame and a name flung high against the stars over Piccadilly—the dream that *might* come true. Many a man and many a maid, who feel they possess a descending lift instead of a stomach, see that name of theirs every night twinkling, glistening, beckoning, making it all seem worth while. That keeps them going.

*   *   *

Heartbreak House

I sat for an hour in a film agent's office which deserves the title of Heartbreak House. Six months ago the crowds of heroes, villains, heroines, and villainesses who clamoured for heroism or villainy became so great that they had to sit four deep down the stairs. Since that time the word has gone forth that there is no work to be had and no point in seeking it ; but still every day they come, hopeful, bright-eyed, the girls all airs and graces, the men eager, self-reliant.

In the waiting-room were six or seven exceedingly pretty fair-haired girls of assorted ages. Some friend had once committed one of the cardinal sins and told them how like Mary Pickford they were. They were now reaping the harvest of this dangerous suggestion. There was an old man with the face of a judge, a young man cut out to be a hero, and a number of vague people who looked in restlessly, and as restlessly went away.

An enormously fat woman occupied the doorway, talking rapidly :

" No fat parts going ? Oh, well, I suppose something 'll turn up some day. Nothing like hope, is there ? And it's not easy for me to keep my weight up with everything so dear these days. Suppose I got thin ? What would I do then ? Oh, what a life, what a life ! "

*　　　*　　　*

The agent entered the room. All the pretty girls pursed their lips and assumed a photographic smile, putting up what they hoped would be a barrage of beauty to demolish all obstacles.

The Heart of London

" Sorry, I can do nothing for you. There's no work ! "

Slowly the smile faded, and each girl looked five years older than girls of that age have any right to look. They fussed a moment with their handbags, brushed imaginary crumbs from their knees, lingered as if hoping against hope that some producer would dash into the office and cry, " Girls, I want you ! " and then, with a sigh, departed ; fawn coats, moleskin, and black coats.

" Pretty awful, isn't it ? " said the agent to me. " You wouldn't think they were out of work. That's part of the game : they must look smart ! "

*   *   *

A big negro put his head round the door, took off a battered bowler, exposed his gums, and said :

" Mornin', boss. Does any guy wanter a good ord'nary nigger ? "

As he went out he came into collision with a tall, pale young man who wore spats but no overcoat. He too, was sent away.

" We get lots like that," said the agent, " well-bred young fellows wearing college ties, who manage to keep their spats white though their shoes probably need soleing. In fact, we get all sorts. But all the men and women who come up here looking as though a thousand a year would be an insult would be grateful for two pound a week. They all look smart."

*   *   *

That is part of their tragedy.

They may be " resting," but they cannot afford to stop acting. The only consolation is that, as everybody knows, luck turns, the darkest hour precedes the dawn, and so on, and so on !

Hope has kept more people alive than all the doctors ever born.

Madonna of the Pavement ◦ ◦ ◦

HOW often in a London street do you try to pierce the mystery of another's life, to visualize the loves, the hates, the joys, the sorrows that have painted lines on some unknown, passing face ?

I saw them in High Holborn. They stood out from the tense, jostling crowd because they seemed to have no object in life, nowhere to go, nothing to do ; they were aimless, lost. They stood out also because they were so poor. Poverty is such a relative thing ; but no man is really poor till life becomes a desert island that gives him neither food nor shelter nor hope. They were such obvious failures at this game of getting and keeping called success. If they had suddenly shouted in pain above the thunder of the passing wheels they could hardly have been more spectacular in their misery, this man, this woman, this child.

He slouched along a few yards in advance of the woman. He looked as though Life had been knocking him down for a long time, then waiting for him to get up so that it might knock him down again. His bent body was clothed in greenish rags and his naked feet were exposed in gashed boots. He was not entirely pathetic. He was the kind of man to whom you would gladly give half a crown to salve your conscience ; but you would never allow him out of sight with your suit-case !

Madonna of the Pavement

She carried her baby against her breast in a ragged old brown cloth knotted round her shoulders. Perhaps she was twenty-five, but she looked fifty because no one had ever taken care of her, or had given her that pride in herself which is necessary to a woman's existence. She had not even the happiness of being wanted or necessary —a condition in which the altruistic soul of woman thrives. This man of hers would obviously be better off without her. She had once been pretty.

The shame of it ! To parade her woman's body draped in rags through streets full of other women in their neat clothes, to meet the pitying eyes of other wives and mothers, and to drag on, tied like a slave, behind this shambling, shifty man. Is there a crucifixion for a woman worse than this ?

* * *

He walked ahead so that she had plenty of time to wonder why she married him. Now and then he would turn and jerk his head, trying to make her quicken her pace. She took no notice, just plodded on in who knows what merciful dullness ?

Then the sleeping child in her old brown shawl awakened and moved with the curious boneless writhing of a young baby. The mother's arms tightened on it and held its small body closer to hers. She stopped, went over to a shop window, and leant her knee on a ledge of stone. She placed one finger so gently into the fold of cloth and looked down into it. . . .

The Heart of London

I tell you that for one second you ceased to pity and you reverenced. Over that tired face of chiselled alabaster, smoothed and softened in a smile, came the only spiritual thing left in these two lives: the beatitude of a Madonna. This same unchanging smile has melted men's hearts for countless generations. The first time a man sees a woman look at his child in exactly that way something trembles inside him. Men have seen it from piled pillows in rooms smelling faintly of perfume, in night nurseries, in many a comfortable nest which they have fought to build to shield their own. No different! The same smile in all its rich, swift beauty was here in the mud and the bleakness of a London street.

They went on into the crowd and were forgotten. I went on with the knowledge that out of rags and misery had come, full and splendid, the spirit that, for good or ill, holds the world to its course.

Two beggars in a London crowd, but at the breast of one—the Future. Poor, beautiful Madonna of the Pavement. . . .

Sword and Cross ⚬ ⚬ ⚬ ⚬

GIRLS were running after omnibuses, lawyers were running after briefs, and reporters were running after things called " stories " as I turned from Fleet Street to enter that little Round Church in the Temple which is one of the most splendid things in London.

Utter peace. A dim, tinted light filtered through the east windows, and at my feet lay the stone figure of Geoffrey de Mandeville, Earl of Essex, bandit and excommunicate. He lies in full chain armour, his shield across his body, his spurs at his heels, and his long sword beside him, just as he might have lain eight hundred and eighty-four years ago, when they found him in the fen country and sent an arrow through his head. What trouble his death must have caused the Templars ! They could not bury him in holy ground till the Pope granted him absolution, so they sealed him up in a lead coffin and hung him on a tree near Holborn. When Rome wiped out his sins they plucked him from the tree and brought him to this little Round Church that was born of the first Crusade.

As I stood over Geoffrey de Mandeville my thoughts raced across Europe, across the Mediterranean, over that sandy yellow waste known as the Desert of Sinai, and on to that city standing high on terraced rock—Jerusalem. Of what else can one think here in the Round Church ? Its roots go back to Robert, Duke of Normandy, Tancred and Bohemund, Godfrey de Bouillon, and that fiery triumvirate, Frederick, Emperor of Germany, Richard Cœur de Lion of England, and Philip Augustus of France.

This quiet little church remembers Saladin; its stones have rung to the chain mail of men who saw the lances of the infidel like a forest against the sky, of men who knew how Frederick Barbarossa came like a storm out of the west to hurl his hosts on the gates of Jerusalem.

Jerusalem. . . . Standing there so near to the roar of London, yet centuries away from it, I recalled white nights on the Mount of Olives, the Holy City spread below over its hills, a dome rising up from violet shadow into the moonlight, a group of cypress trees pointing dark fingers to the stars, and from the faint ribbon of road the trit-trot of a donkey's hoofs going on to Bethany.

The link with Jerusalem is true and straight. It was after they returned from the First Crusade that the Templars built this church to remind them of the round church that guarded the grave of Christ. There are only three others like it in the country, at Cambridge, Northampton, and Little Maplestead, Essex. This church was conceived in Palestine. As I looked at it I recalled the waxen face of a monk whose thin beard was like black silk. I met him in the Church of the Holy Sepulchre in Jerusalem. I had been torn here and there by the confused crowds of pilgrims. I had been mixed up in various sacred processions, I had seen the hungry fervour in which those anxious for salvation had kissed the end of a stick after it had been poked through a hole in an arch so that it might touch a fragment of the Column of the Scourging. And I went on towards the Chapel of the Holy Sepulchre, six foot by six foot, in whose tiny space hang forty-three lamps. Here I saw a poor Greek woman creep in and fall into a torrent of tears on that marble slab which hides the tombstone of Christ. The monk met me outside, such a smooth wax fellow, and led me to a little chapel in which he produced a pair of old spurs and a sword with a hilt shaped like a cross. Godfrey de Bouillon's ! So he said.

I whispered the name in the Round Church. It all links up.

* * *

So quiet it is to-day in the safe keeping of the law. You would never dream that these lawns sloping to the Thames were eight hundred years ago the beginning of that long, hard road to Palestine, the nest of the Templars, those priest warriors who began their history so splendidly poor that two men rode one horse, and ended so richly and dangerously that two kings and the Pope of Rome broke them as three millionaires might smash a trust.

Nothing now remains of all this ancient fire but the Round Church and a few stone crusaders lying with their feet towards the east. A few names linger on, their meaning quite changed. The serjeant-at-law owes his title to the " Fratres Servientes," the serving brothers of the Templars ;

The Heart of London

and the judges' title of " Knight " of the Common Pleas takes us back eight hundred years.

Between the crusaders lying cap-à-pie with Paynim knights beneath their spurred heels, are two brass tablets let into the floor. One is in memory of the members of the Inner Temple, and the other of members of the Middle Temple who laid down their lives in the war.

*　　*　　*

So these crusaders, with eight hundred years dividing them, are rightly commemorated together in this quiet, lovely place, whose atmosphere, once so charged with stress and strife, is now purged by time of all passion, either good or evil. But the ghosts live on, and it would not astonish me to hear that some quiet, harmless lawyer going to his chambers at night down that sloping path past the church met an armed host ready for the march, from whose throats burst like an organ note : " Deus vult ! "

This was the cry that built the Temple, and, spreading out over the land like a flame, fired men's hearts, leading them into the desert in defence of the holy places of Christendom.

Knockout Land ∘ ∘ ∘ ∘

DOWN Whitechapel way is a place famous for dealing out sleep by the fistful twice a week.

None of your six thousand pounds Albert Hall fox-trots here. This is Knockout Land. It is, I imagine, the nearest thing to a bull-fight you will see in this country. Good, hard, slamming fifteen-round contests follow each other, with the ropes trembling and the fight fans howling like a pack of hungry wolves, and two half naked men with strawberry-coloured noses, hitting, gasping, reeling. . . .

A great high hall blue with smoke, steel-girdered at the roof like a railway station. It is packed by a cloth-capped crowd, predominantly Oriental —a crowd of swift murmurs and sudden silences and sharp, instantaneous uproars. Good tempered now, but—O my!—suppose somebody started a row! There is not one woman present. The elegant girls in evening gowns who sit out Albert Hall prize fights have no place here. It is a gathering of fight fans. In the centre under bright, white lights rises the ring. The men in it are like men on a raft floating on a sea of restless, white faces.

Suddenly five or six men near the ring leap to their feet and shout " Five to one on Cohen ! "

The hall becomes thick with wagers. Arms shoot out, men shout, no record is made (except

The Heart of London

that in a keen Hebrew mind), and every one is quite happy about it. Even if the Jew were not so commercially reliable, who would dare to be crooked here !

Look ! The seconds in their white sweaters are busy. Two fighters enter the ring. Their bodies glisten in the light. One is white, the other olive-coloured, Eastern. They square up, crouch, dance round each other, then pat, pat-pat, pat-pat-pat—crack ! A howl goes up from the crowd ! That was a hit ! Smash ! Another one ! Right ! to the ropes ! Back he comes, a little wild, and his opponent is driven away under the speed of his assault. Blows rain on each body, pink patches appear on chests and chins, both men dodge this way and that, a bell rings. Time !

" Chocolates ! " cries a man with a tray.

I want to laugh. A less chocolate-like crowd I have never seen. Jellied eels, perhaps, beer undoubtedly, beefstakes certainly ; but milk chocolate—how astonishing !

Round fifteen ! Both men are all in. They have pounded each other to pulp. I wonder if they can hear the yells and roars of the audience. Their legs drag. They are weak with hitting. You can see what they meant to do as a blow falls short, you can reach out and enter their exhausted minds, sympathize with them in their hazy world as they dog each other to plant the knock-out for which every one is waiting.

Smash ! Right on the chin ! The smashed one reels to the ropes, but comes back for more trouble, with his mouth sagging and something in his

Knockout Land

expression which suggests to me that he is not really here at all, but possibly wandering through some field rich with buttercups, with a little old public-house round the bend in the road. . . . Smash ! He's taken another one ! The scene in his dazed mind changes ! He awakens from some stellar night, and comes alive again out of careering constellations to rush with the desperation of last strength on his opponent. Crack-crack—bang ! Surely the knockout ; surely he cannot stand any more ? His head must be like iron, his jaws like steel.

He reels, his arms drop, his nightmare mind tries to grapple with the padded realities waiting for him, he makes an effort to hit. The other man is now ready to land him one that will lift him off his feet. He is the gladiator standing over him with lifted sword and—no appeal to the amphi-theatre. It is only a question of a second now. Something brutal and masculine inside me desires to see him knocked out ; something weak and feminine inside me wishes it was not necessary.

The victor draws back his head, the muscles ripple along his wet back, he shoots out an arm, and the other man crumples like a marionette at the end of a cut string. He lies in a corner of the ring, moves a leg once, and is still. I feel sure he is dead. In two minutes, with water trickling over his reddened face, he staggers to his feet, smiles a painful, swollen smile, shakes hands with the man who put him to sleep, and gropes out into the obscurity of the yelling crowd.

*   *   *

The Heart of London

" And how much do they get for fighting here ? "

" Oh, thirty-five bob," replies an official.
" Sometimes as much as fifty."

I wonder what our elegant bruisers would
think about it as I make my way out into the
darkness of the wet streets.

Ghosts ✿ ✿ ✿ ✿ ✿ ✿

I OFTEN wonder how many Londoners have been inside No. 13, Lincoln's Inn Fields!

Here we have the most remarkable museum in this and probably any other country. Sir John Soane, the architect who designed the Bank of England, died eighty-eight years ago, and left an instruction in his will that his house, packed with treasures, should be thrown open to the public in the condition in which he left it. The furniture has hardly been moved, the pictures hang in the same positions, and if old Sir John could come back he would enter his library and go over to his desk, hardly knowing that over three-quarters of a century have intervened since he said good-bye to the things he loved with all his heart and soul.

If ever the presence of a dead man printed itself on a house, this is the house. I went there the other day and found the shutters drawn. It was after closing time, but the caretaker asked me inside and courteously took me round.

It was like entering a house when a family is away. I had to pull myself together and realize that this family was eighty-eight years away. There is a certain air about a house whose contents have been arranged by someone who loves it. No museum curator could imitate it. I could, in imagination, see Sir John pottering round with one of his latest treasures, wondering where to put it. He looks in bewilderment. The rooms

The Heart of London

are so crowded! He finds a place, not the best place, but his place; and there it has remained and will remain down the ages.

Another ghost. Lady Soane. Dear woman, she loved these things too, so the biographers say, but it must have given her feminine heart many a twinge to see Roman pillars, gigantic stone fragments from Greek temples, life-size statues, a cast of the Apollo Belvedere, and, at last, the biggest and finest stone coffin ever taken from an Egyptian tomb, enter her home one by one.

" Oh, John," her ghost said, " how full the house is. Where are we going to live ? "

And John, beaming and running his hand over a smooth green bronze, replied, pointing to something new :

" Isn't that perfectly lovely. I think I'll have to knock down the dining-room wall ! "

No woman in the history of housekeeping has ever endured such an overwhelming artistic invasion.

* * *

Sir John began life as the son of a bricklayer. What an encouragement to all collectors of the antique ! As he got on in life he collected more precious things, spent two thousand pounds on an object the British Museum could not afford, and gradually surrounded himself with one of the choicest collections any private individual has possessed.

How many things enthusiasm can accomplish in one lifetime ! It is inspiring to walk through

Ghosts

this old house and realize that everything was collected by one man while he built up his career.

Pictures—notably Hogarth's "The Rake's Progress"—antique gems, bronzes, manuscripts, books, ancient glass, bas-reliefs, the first three folio editions of Shakespeare, and thousands of other things came to him as steel to a magnet. It is not a house : it is a curio shop.

He must have puzzled over space. You would never guess unless you were shown how he made one wall do the work of two or three. He devised walls in many a room which opened like the leaves of a book, each leaf, or side, being hung with pictures. Clever Sir John ; and how Lady Soane must have praised him as the tide of treasure rose higher and higher round her tea-table.

*   *   *

Down in the basement he kept the splendid alabaster coffin of the Pharaoh Seti I, a marvellous thing cut from one solid lump of alabaster. This was the object that Belzoni saw gleaming in the dark tomb in those days when no man could read the weird hieroglyphs with which it is entirely covered.

What a beautiful thing it is. As I looked at it I remembered Belzoni's account of its discovery in that vain, amusing, yet always interesting, "Narrative of the Operations and Recent Discoveries within the Pyramids, Temples, and Tombs and Excavations in Egypt and Nubia," published in 1820. This man's adventures among the tombs of Egypt at a time before Egyptology

was a science are sufficient to make any modern
archæologist lie down and howl with envy at his
opportunities and burn with rage at the opportunities he missed.

After describing the location of the tomb, and
how the debris of three thousand years was
cleared, Belzoni pictures his entry, his progress
through columned halls, his discovery of a rope
that fell to dust when touched. He wandered for
days like a boy in a fairy tale through this tomb,
the most splendid in the Theban Necropolis.

"But the description of what we found in the
centre of the saloon and which I have reserved
till this place," wrote Belzoni, "merits the most
particular attention, not having its equal in the
world, and being such as we had no idea could
exist. It is a sarcophagus of the finest Oriental
alabaster, nine feet five inches long, and three
feet seven inches wide. Its thickness is only two
inches ; and it is transparent when a light is
placed inside of it. It is minutely sculptured
within and without with several hundred figures
which do not exceed two inches in height, and
represent, as I suppose, the whole of the funeral
procession and funeral ceremonies relating to the
deceased. . . . I cannot give an adequate idea
of this beautiful and invaluable piece of antiquity,
and can only say that nothing has been brought
into Europe from Egypt that can be compared
with it."

Just as the reports of the late Lord Carnarvon's
discovery sped through Thebes like wildfire, so
did Belzoni's luck circulate, with the result that

Ghosts

one day the Turkish authorities rode up, headed
by Hamed Aga of Keneh. Then, as now, antiqui-
ties to the native meant simply gold. The Aga,
after glancing vaguely round the tomb, ordered
his soldiers to retire, then, turning to Belzoni he
said :

"Pray where have you put the treasure ? "

"What treasure ? " asked poor Belzoni.

The Aga then told him a story—so like those
in circulation at Luxor in 1923, when it was
rumoured by natives that every woman visitor
to the tomb of Tutankhamen came away with
gold jewellery concealed in her skirts ! Belzoni
denied the rumours of fabulous wealth and of a
reported large golden cock crammed with diamonds
and pearls ! The Aga was crestfallen.

"He seated himself before the sarcophagus,"
wrote Belzoni, "and I was afraid he would take
it into his head that this was the treasure and break
it to pieces to see whether it contained any gold."

Fortunately he did not. He merely delivered
himself of the remarkable observation that the
tomb of Seti I "would be a good place for a harem,
as the women would have something to look at,"
and then, happily for Egyptology and the Soane
Museum, departed.

*   *   *

"Is this place haunted ? " I asked the caretaker,
just to see what he would say.

"No, sir ! " he replied scornfully. "I've heard
noises, but it's mice. There isn't such a thing as
ghosts, believe me."

The Heart of London

But he's wrong; for I saw old Sir John as plainly as anything in those high, leisurely rooms, arranging things, prying into them with a cut crystal, and touching them with fingers that caressed.

Aladdin's Cave ⟡ ⟡ ⟡ ⟡ ⟡

AS I passed through a steel door set in spiked steel railings a hefty commissionaire secretly pressed a bell that gave the alarm downstairs, so that when I appeared two equally hefty commissionaires sprang out and asked me for my password.

No; it was not the Bank of England, or the Tower of London, or Buckingham Palace: it was one of the largest safe deposit vaults in London. Each person who rents a safe there chooses a password—any word he likes; "Annie Laurie," or "Mrs. Jones's Baby," or "Good Queen Anne." Till the commissionaires know him by sight the depositor is held up every time he goes to his safe and is asked to stand and deliver. If he forgets the password he is turned away unless he can prove his identity and his right to unlock his treasures.

Fabulous millions are locked away underground in the safe deposits of London. The companies themselves do not know how much treasure they guard day and night. Now and then the inquiry of an insurance company reveals the fact that a fourteen-inch safe holds a cool million pounds' worth of treasure.

When the commissionaires had looked me over with an expression which inferred that I probably carried on me acetylene blowpipes, a few six-shooters, and a dozen Mills bombs, they called the secretary, who had promised to take me through Aladdin's Cave. The vaults resembled the interior of a great Atlantic liner. In every direction stretched long lit corridors with doors every few feet along them. What doors! Some of them had handles like a giant's dumb-bells and locks like young cartwheels. I imagine that the door of Lord Astor's safe would laugh cheerfully at a howitzer.

The door of one vault was half open. Inside a man was sitting at a table counting diamonds. A pile of white diamonds on a piece of brown paper! Stuck on the wall with the splash of a gum brush was—surprising sight—a coy Kirchner girl adjusting the suspender at the extremity of a long, shining, slim silk leg.

On we went down the corridor, the secretary pointing out the vault of the Duke of This and Lord That, making my head reel with a story of title deeds and heirlooms and treasures beyond price. Another door opened and the owner came out. At first I thought he was about to give us some of the gold plate with which the room was vulgarly full.

" Could you," he said, " lend me a pencil ? "

We gave him one.

On another floor I found the ordinary safes, much less spectacular than the vaults, but, I think, more interesting. Here it is that men and women hide their smaller treasures. You can have quite a nice little safe big enough to take a pair of shoes for twenty-five shillings a year.

I entered an avenue of them, looked at their clumsy hinges and their astonishing locks, wonder-

Aladdin's Cave

ing what mysteries they contain. In how many of them lie letters that would break up homes? In how many are documents that would explain why So-and-So never married? In how many of them are the riches of people whose friends think them penniless? In how many are merely silly things?

" I think the strangest thing we guarded," said the secretary, "was a penny. For thirty years a man paid three pounds a year to guard that penny. No; he was not mad—only superstitious. He believed that if he lost that penny he would have terrible ill-luck. When he first deposited it he was poor, but he died worth a hundred thousand pounds, and his executors then came and took away his mascot."

Another strange treasure was the hoof of a Derby winner. The owner made a fortune from his victory, and when the horse died his wife had the hoof mounted, and they kept it for years in a special safe.

Hundreds of safes in every deposit vault are filled with the jewels of wealthy women. Now and then the owners come and look at them, and sometimes before a ball or a reception they take them away for a night or two. Hundreds also contain the treasures of women who do not seem wealthy. What they contain no one knows. Once when a safe that had not been claimed for twenty years was broken open—it belonged to an elderly spinster—inside were found bundles of faded letters tied up with faded ribbon, all that was left of an old romance.

The Heart of London

What other secrets lie hidden underground in such cold, tiled avenues—what strange human stories that will never be known?

In one of the waiting-rooms I saw an ancient man with a white beard. He was sitting over the contents of his safe, feebly fingering documents and poring over them, his nose almost touching the papers. The sight of him roused questions. How easy to write a dozen speculations about him, his life, and his little tray full of musty deeds and letters. . . .

* * *

Outside over the wet pavements hurried the men and women of London, unconscious that beneath their feet lay millions and—mystery.

That Sad Stone ◦ ◦ ◦ ◦ ◦

IN two thousand years' time will there be
brambles growing on Ludgate Hill, I wonder,
and will a shepherd graze his sheep in Piccadilly
Circus ? It happened to Thebes and Carthage. . . .

If the tamarisks should come back to town I
desire to be reincarnated at that time in order
that I may join in archæological speculation on
the fragment of an extinct animal (" probably a
lion ") dug up on the site of Trafalgar square ! It
would also be jolly to reconstruct the plan of Bush
House on the strength of three window-sills, a
lift bell, and a typewriter key. There are great
days in store for those who will shake up our dust
and worry our ghosts, and even attempt to discover
our gods. I can see Macaulay's New Zealander
having the time of his life among the ruins of
London ; and surely one of his most splendid
adventures will take place at the base of Cleopatra's
Needle. Did you know that beneath this famous
stone is buried a kind of Victorian Tutankhamen's
treasure, placed there to give some man of the
future an idea of us and our times ? Did you
realize that the London municipal authorities
could do anything so touching ?

Under the obelisk sealed jars were placed in
1878 containing a man's lounge suit, the complete
dress and vanities of a woman of fashion, illustrated papers, Bibles in many languages,
children's toys, a razor, cigars, photographs of

the most beautiful women of Victorian England, and a complete set of coinage from a farthing to five pounds. So the most ancient monument in London stands guard over this modernity, rather like an experienced old hen, waiting for Time to hatch it.

Poor sad old stone. . . .

*　　*　　*

I went down to look at it yesterday when the Thames, in full tide, dancing in the sunlight, was giving the Embankment great slapping kisses. Tugs were chugging upstream with their ugly duckling barges; and the jet-black finger of Ancient Egypt pointed to the sky, so slim and beautifully proportioned, so tall that when I looked up it seemed to be falling against the wheeling clouds.

Two little boys were riding a sphinx. Men and women stopped, looked up at the monument, saw the pale sunlight finding its way into those funny little carvings, a few moved round to the rear of the platform and gazed with open mouths, seeing an incomprehensible stone, wondering about it perhaps, maybe feeling that there was a story behind it somewhere, somehow.

A story? Heavens! What a story. Shall I tell you what I saw as I stood there with the tramcars speeding past and the criss-cross traffic busy on its way?

*　　*　　*

I saw a great tunnel of Time three thousand

That Sad Stone

four hundred years long. Imagine the time that separates us to-day from the Spanish Armada and then *multiply it by ten* : that is almost three thousand and four hundred years. London was unknown. We were probably beating our wives in the Thames marshes and eating an occasional aunt. Greece was unborn, and there was no Rome on the Seven Hills. But Egypt had thrashed its way through the mumps and measles of civilization and was already ancient. In this distant blaze of light moved epicures and artists, soldiers and priests, and in the great palace of Thebes sat the most powerful man in that time of the world, the Pharaoh Thothmes III, Lord of the Two Lands, giver of life and death.

And Pharaoh decided to perpetuate his greatness in the eye of Time. In other words, he probably remarked after dinner one night : " I want obelisks for the temple at Heliopolis. That pylon looked rather bare, I thought, the last time I was there. You might see to it, will you ? "

Whereupon chariots were harnessed and messengers sped south to the red-hot granite quarries of Assuan.

*   *   *

Now see the architect drawing the shape of Cleopatra's Needle in the virgin rock. See hundreds of naked backs bent over the stone, pounding, pounding, pounding month after month in the savage heat with no tools but hard balls of dolomite ; and the whips crack over the sweating bodies and flicker in the heat and hiss like the tongues of serpents.

In a year the whim of Pharaoh is bashed from the quarry in blood and tears. His titles are set upon it, and it stands, painted and glorious, fronting the Temple of the Sun in Heliopolis. On its tip is a cap of electrum that catches the sun, so that travellers in the desert looking towards the city of On see a pillar with a fire blazing upon it. . . . Look!

A cloud of dust; and in the heart of it gilded chariots. The white horses are pulled up on their haunches, the nodding ostrich plumes on their head collars rise and fall, the fan bearers come forward, the troops stand at ease, and above the kneeling priests is the Pharaoh, that ancient superman, inspecting his monument from a burnished car.

"Quite good. The god is pleased."

* * *

Time passes. Moses, who was a priest in Heliopolis, sees the obelisk every day. The frogs of the Plagues hop and chirrup on its plinth. Over a hundred years pass, and Rameses the Great, who loved himself dearly, carves his name on the column, usurping it. A thousand years pass, and it is moved to Cleopatra's capital at Alexandria. Here it survives four great empires. Thrones rock and fall, dynasties fade like mists. The world changes. Two thousand years pass by, and a new race of men come to power. They pick Cleopatra's Needle out of the sand, enclose it in a huge steel cylinder, give it a deck, a keel, a rudder, put a crew aboard and tug it across the sea towards England. Prosperous winds favour the voyage for the first few weeks; then, in the dreaded Bay of Biscay, Cleopatra's Needle pitches with such violence that the tug's captain cuts her adrift with her crew aboard her. How different from her last voyage three thousand years previously, when the Egyptian slaves floated her on the sunlit Nile for the delight of Pharaoh! As she rolls and tosses five sailors from the tug volunteer to go out to the abandoned obelisk ship. They are swept under and are drowned. Eventually the Cleopatra's crew are saved and the tug watches her drift away over the stormy seas. Sixty days pass and then news is received that Cleopatra's Needle was tugged into Vigo by a ship whose owners received two thousand pounds for their services. Eventually, tugged by an M.P.'s yacht the Egyptian stone arrives in England.

Here, forty-seven years ago, they placed it beside a cold, grey river, and some unknown hand penned the following epitaph to it in the morning :

This monument as some supposes
Was looked on in old days by Moses ;
It passed in time to Greeks and Turks,
And was stuck up here by the Board of Works.

* * *

Here it has remained beside the Thames, with the last great adventure still in store. One night the wrath of Ra, the fury of Set, the god of evil,

The Heart of London

descended like thunderbolts from a dark sky. Chips of the granite pediment flew away. The plinth was bruised as a city is bruised in war, and overhead in the shaft of a searchlight lay a silver fish in the sky—a fish that hummed like a hornet and laid most devilish eggs. What a strange night for ancient Egypt. . . .

*   *   *

Sad, cold stone—the saddest monument in all London. We are killing it. It was once red granite. Now it is coal black and its glory is being eaten away year by year. Forty-seven years of London have done it greater hurt than the three thousand years that went before. It did not deserve this ; for round it centres the splendour and glory of the past and under its feet is a message for the future.

And it seems to me that its experienced black finger is pointing to something which may make you laugh or cry.

Sun or Snow   ∘   ∘   ∘   ∘   ∘

VICTORIA STATION is every morning the
scene of a daily romance—the departure of
the Continental boat expresses. When the fog
comes and the rain and the driving sleet, and every
Londoner loathes London just a little, I can
extract a certain pale kind of pleasure by buying
a penny platform ticket and watching other people
start off to the snow or the sun.

I can never decide whether the act of extracting
enjoyment from other people's luck is the lowest
or the highest form of fun. There is always a
sting in the tail of it.

*   *   *

When you love travel, and have lost count of
the number of times the chocolate-coloured Pull-
mans have whirled you through Kent to the edge
of the sea and on to far places, this morning
assembly of travellers shakes you to the heart.
You know what is in store for them. You follow
them down to Dover ; you see them in the swift
Channel boat ; you hear the blue-bloused porters
of Calais crying " Soixante-dix, m'sieu. I meet
you at ze douane ! " You visualize the idiotic
fight in the French Customs ; you see the long
Paris Rapide waiting with steam up, the wrinkled
old Frenchwomen in white caps and knitted black
shawls who sell fruit, and you hear the funny
little penny whistle like a child's trumpet that

The Heart of London

sends this great train racketing and thundering through France, or Basle and Switzerland, or Marseilles, and then—oh, marvellous far places in Africa !

Which is more wonderful ? To awaken at the Swiss frontier with snow muffling a cotton-wool world of chasms and peaks, or to awaken in the sunlight of Southern France to a glimpse of the blue Mediterranean ?

*   *   *

That wide, hedgeless plain with its silver-grey olive trees, its red-roofed houses, and its vignettes of rustic activity ; little men in fields walking behind the plough, at stable doors bringing out a solemn, ragged mule, give me that. And give me, too, the ever-recurring joy of the uncomfortable swinging French *wagon restaurant* full of various people : Englishmen who look so comically English as soon as they cross the Channel, Frenchmen whose black spade beards cascade over white table-napkins which they tuck into their collars before they devour their food with Gallic avidity, and the good-looking Parisienne with her carmine mouth and her finicky, much-manicured hands breaking bread and salting meat while her big, emotional eyes sweep over and beyond the bald heads of appraising British husbands.

" Liqueur, m'sieu ? "

The man with the tray of little bright bottles staggers up and, notable sight, the elderly virgin of some distant vicarage sips an unusual brandy. Marvellous France !

Sun or Snow

So, knowing all this so well, I watched the boat train crowds with the keenest enjoyment the other morning. There were girls who would be tumbling about in the snow before many days were gone, or sitting in the palish summer of the Riviera in white, pleated skirts. There went the hardened traveller with the well-worn rucksacks and the skis, the excited, flushed traveller making a first journey, and—lucky fellow—a man with a white pith helmet over his arm.

Nothing is more awkward to pack than a pith helmet. Even socks and shaving tackle will not sit comfortably in it. When carried with an air it advertises the fact that you are not a mere Swiss fan or a poor Riviera lizard, but an honest-to-goodness traveller, possibly even an explorer. In the Channel boat people will look at you as you bear this symbol of the sun on your arm. You will stand out above all others. Perhaps in the bar some one will say :

" Going far ? " and you can flick the ash of your cigarette carelessly and say :

" No ; only to Timbuctoo ! "

A great thing is a sun helmet !

Then there was the lady of quality off to Monte Carlo, with trunks full of dresses, and one trunk lightly packed to contain more dresses which she will accumulate in Paris. There was a pale woman who had obviously been ordered South. Her husband stood beside the Pullman door telling her to take great care of herself and get well, and just before the train left he shyly, like a boy, gave her a little packet in white tissue paper, which she opened, and the tears came into her eyes as she held the small jeweller's box in her hand. Yes ; there are such husbands !

All the time the cosy lamplit tables of the Pullman cars gradually filled. At one a man turned to the weather report, where under a weird map of barometric pressure he would read about the Channel crossing ; at another a woman gazed thoughtfully through the menu wondering if it would be wise to eat a grilled sole.

*　　　*　　　*

Sharp to the last second of the minute the Continental boat express slipped out of Victoria with its load of people in search of health and pleasure. A flutter of handkerchiefs, a turn away, and the tail coach disappeared with those squat mail boxes on it which are lifted by a crane into the hold of the ship and lifted out in France, fixed on a railway wagon, and consigned to the G.P.O. in Paris.

As the boat express went off the diminishing grind of its wheels seemed to sing to me of olive yards and orange groves and long white roads in sunlight, and, somewhere far down in the south, a ship. . . .

Romantic Mutton ～ ～ ～ ～

SUPPOSE you were walking down that delicious slope of Piccadilly, the Green Park rails on your left, and suddenly you saw Sir Claude, the wicked young squire, chucking a shepherdess under the chin while he slapped his riding boots with a hunting crop. Suppose . . .

This happens! Turn down Whitehorse Street, and in two seconds bald heads in club windows, pretty sandy-legged ladies, the flood stream of omnibuses, are forgotten. They have never existed. They are two hundred comfortable years off in the womb of Time. You stand in the eighteenth century, in a London of maypoles and gallantry and much sly sin, of coaches and caval-cades, inn parlours and buxom serving wenches. Even your spats feel elegant. You desire to snap an ivory snuffbox, to wave a fine cambric handker-chief, and to kiss a good-looking chambermaid. Odds truth, sir, you are under the influence of Shepherd Market! At any moment my Lord Maxbridge may turn the corner on the arm of Sir Timothy Strophe, poet and wit, and you will, of course, stand, leaning on your ebony cane, promising to look in at the Cocoa Tree to-night and to join my lord later (bow) at his box at Vauxhall. And did you hear what the Prince said last night of Lady T., and how young Charles H. took it ? And did you know that Captain X. lost nine hundred guineas at cards on a single throw at White's, and that the Marquis de St. A. has sent his seconds to Lord M., and that Sir Richard T. has been black-balled at Brooks'? Gad, sir!

That, at least, is how it takes me!

Looked at with the eyes only, Shepherd Market reveals itself as a queer, haphazard warren of streets packed with little shops whose onions overflow on the pavement, whose cabbages sometimes collapse into the gutter, whose fish and meat are much in evidence. Here you have the atmosphere of the Pantiles and the formation of any square in any old county town you care to remember.

This is picturesque. Behind any grand modern street you seem to see a surveyor or an architect bending over a blue paper, drawing straight lines. These shops and squares have grown up naturally, as a clump of flowers grows—some here, some there; some big, some small. What splendid individuality.

Here, within a stone's throw of Piccadilly, shop-keepers display big galvanized dust-bins on the pavement. You might be in Salisbury market-place. A china shop sells pretty little teapots of the kind which spinster ladies drive into Ipswich to procure on market day. All manner of antique shops sleep in the shadows. In one window I saw really good china, in others Georgian silver and rushlight holders.

It is Georgian or Victorian, according to taste. You can people the uneven pavements with ghosts of your own choosing. No matter how many gallants and dames you discover, there are a few later characters whom you expect to meet at every turn. The colonel's wife! Where is she? You look round anxiously. She should be walking stiffly round with her cane, a couple of Sealyhams rolling affectionately at the hem of her tailor-made skirt. The bishop's lady, too, a tall, lined woman in a religious black hat; the dean's daughter, romantic and anæmic and addicted to green velvet; Lady Potts, from "The Hall," in a dog-cart, large, florid, and suspiciously golden; the three hefty unmarriageable daughters of the major-general (retired), with their bicycles; the pretty wife of a junior subaltern—all the stock characters of an English cathedral city or garrison town.

Instead, so strange is this rural atmosphere, go London folk, smart women from flats in Curzon Street, and men passing through on their way to their clubs.

*　　*　　*

How did this patch become insulated from the fierce current of London life? I will tell you. They used to hold a fair here every May as far back as Edward I. Then, in 1738, a Mr. Shepherd built a cattle market on the spot. The butchers' shops had theatres on the second storeys, so that the dwarfs and drolls and vagabonds might in fair-time amuse the crowds. In 1750 so many regrettable things happened here that the fair was suppressed as a public scandal. (It must have been very wicked!)

So this is the heritage of our Shepherd Market,

this concentrated essence of old England set down within sound of the wheels of Mayfair. If you visit it, notice how the old butchers' shops linger on, relics of the Shepherd Market of 1738. I imagine that there is here more prime Welsh mutton to the square yard than in any other street in London.

Romantic mutton!

London Lovers ∽ ∽ ∽ ∽ ∽

WHEN I was walking along the Embankment
on a path of pale sun, I saw a young man
and a young woman leaning over the grey stone
watching the river. There were white gulls
wheeling, and the river was high ; and this man
and this woman were very still and intent. When
I stood beside them I found they were not looking
at the river, they were looking at the Future !

Under cover of their leaning arms they were
holding hands. They were in the last stage of
love, their eyes like fields full of moon-calves.
His clothes were Sundayfied and his boots were
new and brown—the colour of a retired Indian
general.

Her hat had been made at home in a hurry.
And they were standing there lost in the illimitable
wonder of each other. They were not in London.
They were in that aerial country on the boundaries
of paradise, from which such men and women
descend to a small red box in the suburbs and the
current price of eggs.

I could compose their imaginary dialogue easily.
I could tell you that he whispered about the fifteen
pounds in the bank, that they murmured daringly
of banns, and an oak suite on the instalment
system. But, no ! They said nothing, because
they had reached that condition when words cease
to capture meaning.

And I thought how well worth writing of are

The Heart of London

the lovers of London, the ordinary little lovers, whose sitting-out places are the parks, whose adventures are omnibus rides to Kew, whose extravagances are tea and buns.

Every Sunday they walk London. Every week-day you can see them in the solemn City snatching a half-hour at luncheon, she with an index finger purpled by a new ribbon, he very clerkly and correct. And you must never think them mean when, having watched each other eat steak and kidney pie as if they were sitting at a mystery play, they call for separate bills.

He pays his one and threepence and she pays hers. How significant that is. Had he been philandering with her they would have had a far nicer luncheon in a very much nicer restaurant, and he would have carelessly ordered an ice and ended up recklessly with coffee and perhaps even a sinister *crème de menthe*. And he would have paid the bill, giving her the impression it was a mere nothing. She would not be allowed to know that his hand, groping mysteriously in his pocket, was trying desperately to discover whether there was enough left for seats in a cinema, whether— dash it all !—that little coin in the dark of his slender pocket was a penny or a much-hoped-for half-crown.

Ah, a bad sign. The road to bankruptcy is paved with boasting and insincerity and such little showings off ! Let him once discover the Girl, and then with life imminent they get down to truth, and she discovers that he is not the lordly thing he pretended to be, that he is not earning a

London Lovers

splendid fiver a week but a solemn two pounds ten. Crisis ? Oh, dear, no !

There then begins a wrestle with a skeleton disguised as a bank account. They both stand guard over it. An extra packet of cigarettes is a betrayal, a reckless splash at a movie is a crime against a new little home that exists nowhere but in two hearts. So he pays his bill and she pays hers, and all the time the modest little pile grows, leading them to those helpful organizations which give two hundred pounds worth of property for ten per cent down and the rest over eternity.

*　　*　　*

They are happy, are these little lovers of London ; as all honest, simple things are happy. No great winds of passion or ambition blow like storms in their hearts. They wish to escape from their surroundings into something which is their very own. They dream of the little house, just like every other little house in the row, and they dream of locking the front door on life and opening their arms to each other.

In the great hive of London you can see them meeting, hungrily snatching a moment from their separate labours which are just a means to an end. In the City she comes, lighting his heart with her beauty, and she goes, leaving him feeling that the light has been turned off inside him. At Kew in lilac time you will find them in sweet green avenues ; the red buses bear them and their Dream to country places ; and one day you will meet them in a tube train bending self-consciously over a furniture catalogue. . . .

*   *   *

Dante and Beatrice came out of their dream beside the Thames and walked away. Dante's new boots squeaked. Arm-in-arm they went along the sun path, two ordinary little actors in the great play, with that stillness about them that suggests how full two hearts can be.

If one could only peep into their lives again in ten years' time. That, however, is tempting Fate.

In Uncle's Shop   *o*   *o*   *o*   *o*

OUTSIDE on its rusty supports hung the sign of the proud Medici—three gold balls. Inside the pawnbroker's shop nothing was proud, except perhaps a grandfather clock that stood in a corner like an old aristocrat who has buttoned his coat, cocked his hat, and decided to go down hill with an air. For the rest—just junk lingering in this sordid, waiting-room atmosphere to be reclaimed and taken home. I looked at it and saw it as junk ; then I looked again, knew that some of it had been hard to part with, was, in fact, transmuted by affection so that its very frayed unloveliness brought tears to their eyes. Those cheap, badly-made china shepherdesses designed to simper across a mantelpiece at the girlish gallant whose flirtations salute was ruined because the hand that once held his hat had vanished —how remarkable that anyone had made them, how remarkable that anyone had cared sufficiently to buy them ! There they were in the pawnshop, and perhaps some poor woman scraping up four-pence interest to keep them hers, gazing at her bare mantelpiece, longing for their sugary smiles, the cheap, conventional romance of them. . . .

*   *   *

" Something'll happen soon," said the pawn-broker to me. " You just have to wait."

So I waited for comedy or pathos in the dim

The Heart of London

crowded shop that smelt of undusted china and old boots. Beyond the stacked window—so full of clocks and fractious bronze horses, of watches and silly shaped silver vases—I saw a busy London district; people passing and repassing, tramcars at congested cross-roads, omnibuses, women shopping and stopping to talk, their baskets over their arms. I became aware of a man in a blue overcoat examining the window.

" He's an old hand at 'popping' things," said the pawnbroker.

" You know him then ? "

" Never seen him before ; but I can tell."

" How ? "

" Well, just watch the way he's going over my stock. I bet he's sized up every blessed thing in the window. It's the jewellery he's interested in. He's wondering if I'm overstocked with gold bracelets. See, he's counting them. He's not sure. He's coming in. You listen ! "

The man in the blue overcoat entered, and spoke in a firm, rather condescending manner.

" Look here," he said, " would you care to give me anything on this ? I shall be getting it out some day."

He threw on the counter a gold bangle.

" Ten shillings," said the pawnbroker.

" Dirty dog ! " said the man, and walked out.

" Old X. round the corner'll give him a pound for it," said the pawnbroker calmly. " He's rather low in bangles."

A well-dressed young man in a great hurry rushed in and detached a watch from his chain :

In Uncle's Shop

"I've never done this before!" he said. "But I want some money quickly."

It was a good watch, thin as a wafer. Gold.

"Two pounds?"

"Right!" Off he rushed.

All sorts came in, reflected the pawnbroker, you could never tell. Some needed money desperately and some just wanted it at the moment. Young men pawn watches to pay the landlady, to back a horse, to take a girl out to dinner, to stave off a creditor, to buy food. A decent coat disguises motives. Sometimes a "real lady," who had been playing too much bridge, "popped" something really worth while, and always in a quiet shop like this; sometimes "flashy" people came with diamonds, and then you had to keep your eyes open.

* * *

In came a little wisp of a woman. She put sixpence on the counter. I noticed her thin wrists and the criss-cross grimed lines on her fingers. She called the pawnbroker "sir." When she had gone he showed me the article on which she was paying interest. It was a small box with mother-of-pearl diamonds set in the lid, many of them missing. She had been paying interest for two years.

In every pawnshop there are thousands of things like this box: links with happier days perhaps, things which sentiment enthrones in the heart. I could build up a dozen stories round this box: the gift of a mother, a dead husband, a son ? A Pandora's box full of the winds of old happiness ? I leave it to your imagination.

* * *

Then, at the tail of a number of people, some of whom were obviously pledging their overcoats for a long drink of beer, came a woman with dark rings round her eyes, and she said :

"My husband's ill . . . very ill . . . and I must, I simply must. . . ."

She wrestled unhappily with her left hand and placed on the counter a plain gold ring. . . .

"That was horrible," I said.

"Look here," replied the pawnbroker. He opened a drawer and ran his fingers through a pile of wedding rings. "They keep them to the end," he explained, "but——"

"I understand. I've seen quite enough. I think I'll be moving on."

Horsey Men o o o o o

HAVE you ever calculated how much respect you can buy with a sudden half-crown?

A railway porter will give you quite a lot, an hotel porter will unbend slightly, and under its influence even a taxi-cab driver, if the fare is about seven and sixpence, will appear fairly human. But if you want your money's worth, go briskly into Aldridge's or Tattersall's on the day of a horse sale, walk up to a man who wears a white jacket and holds a whip, give him half a crown and say at the same time: "Selling any hunters to-day?" You know at once that you have made a hit. As an American would say, he reacts immediately. In one swift eye-sweep he has made a mental note of you; he knows the kind of horse he thinks you ride, the way you will ride it, and so on. He looks knowing, a quality shared by all men even remotely connected with the sale of horseflesh, and, slightly closing one eye, he whispers:

"Come with me, sir!"

* * *

You are in a stable facing the posteriors of many horses. The hunters, the aristocrats of the sale, are boxed together in a corner, but there are big hefty carthorses and sturdy hacks of every kind. You look down the catalogue: "Bay mare, has been ridden side-saddle and astride." What lovely girl rode her side-saddle

and astride, you wonder, called her " Nelly," and
came to the stable every morning with a lump of
sugar ?

" Look out, sir ! " says your admirer, as he
taps Nelly's hocks lightly with his whip, causing
her to swerve round and show you a dilated pupil
and a suspiciously poised near-side hoof. " Now,
sir, that's your 'oss, that is ! "

You don't deceive him. You don't explain
that you are only doing this for fun, to while
away a weary hour, to banish ennui. On he goes,
a natural-born auctioneer. She's your weight,
she is, and she has a lovely mouth, she has, and
he wouldn't be surprised if she was a marvellous
jumper, he wouldn't. . . .

For one half-crown and a minimum amount
of attention you can spend hours with this man
prodding flanks, feeling hocks, and running your
hand over withers, but the best thing to do
is to run down the horses, call them " rough
stuff," and go off into the yard where they are
having a sale.

Now horse fancying has created a unique type
of man familiar to you in the country, but never
seen in London except at these sales. When you
regard them *en masse* the effect is remarkable.
You feel that if a coach-and-four suddenly drove
in they could all take seats and drive out looking
like one of Cruikshank's illustrations in Dickens.
People would say : " What are they advertising ? "

They are horse-faced, thin, bow-legged, and
some of them actually suck straws—most difficult
things to find in London these days if you contract

Horsey Men

the habit. They wear little fawn coats with pearl buttons and tight little gaiters well up on the tops of their boots ; and they walk with a roll.

You have seen a wicked man in a night club on the movies look at the heroine. He screws up his eyes and looks straight at her ankles, and then slowly insults her with his eyes as his gaze ascends. These horsey men look at horses just like that : their eyes glance contemptuously at hoofs, linger sneeringly on fetlocks, wander disparagingly over other parts of the anatomy, then they say : " Wind sucker," or " Roarer," or " Eats her bedding," and light a cigar.

*   *   *

Into the ring is led a chestnut mare.

She is a lovely thing, and you can tell by the way she trembles and tosses her head that she is not having a good time. She does not understand. There are many things she does understand. She understands the man into whose waistcoat it is so good to place her moist muzzle, she understands the slightest move of him in the saddle, and she loves to obey when, feeling the faintest pressure of his knees, she breaks into a canter over soft grass, and falls again into a trot, to find his hand patting her sleek neck.

Why isn't he here ? He has never let others take control of her before ! In a moment, no doubt, he will come and drive all these men off ; and then they will go out together to their own place as they have always done. She looks round. Whinnies. But her man is not there.

The Heart of London

Then the auctioneer, a little fellow in a silk hat, explains that this splendid chestnut mare, sound in wind and limb and eye, is being sold to save her summer keep. The horse fanciers come a step nearer, they whisper, they begin to bid. . . .

Bang ! The hammer descends. The little chestnut mare starts suddenly as if she knew that she had got a new master.

* * *

They lead her out under the wide arch of the livery stable, and in the proud tossing of her head and her backward looks you seem to read : " Where is that man of mine, and why—why doesn't he come ? "

From Bow to Ealing ∂   ∂   ∂   ∂

I HAVE realized one of my first ambitions. In the dark engine cab of an Underground train I have shot like a comet through light and darkness, the glittering tail of the train thundering behind packed with people on their way from Bow to Ealing.

A bell rang. The driver looked out over the track where three gleaming steel rails met in a point outside a tunnel. He pulled over a lever and the train started. It was the strangest sensation. I forgot the six packed coaches at the back of us. I forgot the cargo of calm newspaper-reading men and novel-reading girls which we were carrying across London. In the semi-darkness of the driver's cab an ordinary Underground journey had become strangely adventurous and exciting.

The driver accelerated. His pointer moved round a dial, and the train answered his small movements, gathering speed and noise. I was conscious only of being in the grip of a tremendous force that was hurling us over those three gleaming rails. We took the tunnel at a good thirty-five miles an hour, and the noise we made changed to a hollow roar! I could feel the train swerve and rock slightly as we rounded a curve; but I could see nothing save here and there a green light close to the ground. If you can imagine that you are tied to a projectile shot from a gun in the night,

133

you have an idea of driving an electric train through a tunnel.

In the underground blackness stations show first as a faint yellow glow cut across by the jet-black semicircle of the tunnel. The next second you can see their curving rows of lights; they straighten out, and then the platform at which you will pull up lies level as a knife edge before you. Mark Lane . . . Mansion House . . . Blackfriars . . . Temple . . . Charing Cross.

Charing Cross is big. As you sweep in the driver has time to collect a lightning series of snapshots! A bookstall, a cigarette booth, lit and yellow, a pretty girl coming down the steps carrying a bag, a fussy old lady asking a ticket inspector how to get to Baron's Court, and a sudden stir and interest of Ealing-bound people who detach themselves from the crowd of waiting passengers. Just a flash! All seen in the fraction of a second! Bells ring down the train. A loud one clangs in the engine cab. And off you go again through the blackness towards Victoria.

Few things are more uncanny in mechanical London than the system of automatic signalling which permits a chain of electric trains to move over the same line at minute intervals with no chance of a collision.

Little green lights beckon you on, telling you the way is clear. As you pass them red lights at your back change to green, beckoning on the train behind; and so it is all the way along. Now and then you meet a red light. You stop! The light changes to green. On you go! The marvellous thing is that if, in a moment of colour blindness, you tried to override a red light your train would correct you. It would refuse to go on!

At Kensington we shot out into the open air. Gaily, madly, we raced over the shining rails, marvellously, so it seemed to me, taking a sharp bend, smoothly continuing along the straight. It was like flying without the perpetual anxiety of flight. Once, with the awful insolence of the cocksure, I thought the driver had erred.

"Good Lord!" I said. "That was a red light, and *you've gone on*!"

Instead of kicking me out on the metals, as he should have done, he smiled and remarked:

"Wrong signal! That red light governs the loop line!"

Safe! On we thundered triumphantly Ealingwards, with the green lights smiling a benediction on us, telling us that the next ahead was at least a minute ahead, telling the next behind that we, in our turn, were sixty seconds on the right side of safety.

"Do you ever get bored with driving the Ealing express?"

"No," replied the driver, "I like it! I wanted to do this ever since I became a conductor. Most conductors want to be drivers. The first time you take a train out alone is what you might call a bit of excitement, but it soon wears off."

"You don't feel as though you were flying?"

"No, you soon lose that feeling."

"You never get the wind up?"

The Heart of London

" No, you can't go wrong if you keep your eyes open and your repair bag in good order ! "

* * *

In a cabin where a signalman kept his eyes on an illuminated map over which little black snakes were crawling—trains coming and trains gone—I met an inspector who had been on London's electric railways for over thirty years !

" The changes I've seen ? " he said. " Yet it's marvellous what we did in the old days. Do you know that we used to take eighty thousand people a day to exhibitions in the old steam trains ? I'm not saying that we wern't a bit packed and a few children on the rack, but—we did it ! Now, of course, everything is bigger, quicker, and better, and—you can have the good old days ! I remember them and prefer these !

" Why, bless my soul, in the good old days we had to have a regular baby hunt nearly every night under the seats of the old trains. Anybody who didn't want a baby seemed to leave it in the Underground."

* * *

I bought a ticket like any ordinary unenlightened passenger and went back to London in a " smoker " with my thoughts straying to the man in the engine cab ahead, sitting there with his eyes glued to the little *crème de menthe* lights that tell him he can fly and thunder on through the darkness.

Marriage ◦ ◦ ◦ ◦ ◦ ◦

A STRIPED awning leads to the church. A narrow strip of scarlet carpet runs from kerb to porch. Policemen hold back the crowd.

Women—always women; and in such numbers, too, and in such remarkable variety. The lily livered misanthrope on a passing omnibus growls: "Another wretched wedding. . . . What women see in them I cannot imagine." Of course he cannot. Women with their relentless grip on essential realities, see in them the work of the world, the justification of all living—but, naturally, they do not reason it out like that. They go to "see the bride," or, dare I say, to see themselves as the bride, either as they once were or as they hope to be.

How remarkably they gather! At one moment the street is normal save for that tell-tale scarlet strip; the next, as a swarm gathers out of the blue sky, so gather the wedding fans, ready, if need be, to prod a policeman in the ribs with an umbrella in order to watch another woman walk through a wedding-ring into a home. . . .

Shall we join the ladies?

* * *

"Steady on there. Don't push."

That is the policeman. There is a surge and writhing of this solid mass of womanhood.

The Heart of London

" Officer, could you stand just a little. . . .
Thank you."

" 'Ere, Robert, can't you move your fat self ?
I'm only a little one."

All kinds of women : Kensington and Balham
and Clerkenwell ; virgins, matrons, and grand-
mothers ; some happy, some, no doubt, unhappy.
What does that matter ? Another bride is step-
ping out into life with the future in her eyes, and joy
and sorrow presiding over her marvellous destiny.

*　　*　　*

" Who is it ? "

" Lady Agatha Penwhistle ! "

Not you see, " Who is *he* ? " What does *he*
matter ? Half the women have never heard of
Lady Agatha. To them she is not Lady Agatha.
She is something far more important : she is a
bride ; she is—Everywoman.

In the dark arch of the church porch a certain
anticipatory liveliness is noted. Pink young men
in morning clothes, white gardenias in their button-
holes, fuss helplessly, asking each other whispered
questions, pointing, hesitating, muddling. Marriage is a bad day for young brothers. The boys
at the porch have been tumbling over pews and
mixing up the bride's guests with those who owe
allegiance to the bridegroom. It has been a fearful sweat for them. The sight of Sis at the altar,
too, was pretty awful. Of course, George is an
awfully decent cove and all that ; but still, you
know . . . so small she was, and so pathetic
in white, kneeling there. . . .

Marriage

One of the young men runs down the steps and officiously opens the door of a limousine in whose silver brackets shine white carnations. The crowd watches every movement. He blushes under the scrutiny. Silly asses, they are! Then as he runs back the doors are flung wide. Suddenly the church vibrates like a great cat purring. The stones seem to rock, as, with a crash, the hysterical triumph of Mendelssohn bursts forth and goes galloping down the wind like a messenger. There are people crowding round the porch. She is coming. . . . She, the eternal, unchanging, marvellous She!

Look, there is a movement in the porch, and then . . . " Oooh, isn't she lovely!"

The Girl in White!

Her veil flung back, her straight, slim form moving down the steps, the white satin gleaming as she moves, her bouquet against her breast, and her silver toes peeping in and out from beneath her gown. She smiles.

" Good luck, my dear!"

A swift turn of her head. Who said that to her? Her eyes brim, for it was very lovely. She gazes over the women's faces—those, at this time, generous women's faces.

So she passes.

*   *   *

As she goes the women put away their handkerchiefs, for they have all been crying a little, some with joy and some out of the depths of knowledge.

The Heart of London

To all of them standing there She represented That Which Once Was, That Which Might Have Been, That Which May Be ; and something more— oh, much more. For that brief second she was the Ideal. She was Happiness.

I think also that when the older women found themselves in tears they were seeing through a glass darkly, through the glass of this girl's life, and in their hearts they knew that, come weal, come woe, they had seen a sister at the pinnacle of her life.

* * *

" Good luck, my dear ! "

Kings and Queens ∘ ∘ ∘ ∘

NELL GWYNNE must have had some trying moments. When she fell into a red-haired woman's rage facing Charles II with clenched hands, Charles probably stood there looking at her just as he looks at the few people who from time to time gaze at him in the Westminster Abbey waxwork show.

Women hate to be looked at like that, whether the man who looks is a king or is merely someone else's husband. "Now, Nelly!" he seems to be saying. "Now, Nelly!" Cold, distant, on the apex of his pyramid of superiority, with his sallow, cynical face framed in its cascade of curls, how mad he must have made her—and all the others —for women who permit themselves hysterics do detest having them against a human granite quarry. That sad, superior Stuart eye, that heavy, drooping mouth, that thin, supercilious pencil line of a moustache etched straight over, but a little above, his upper lip. So contemptuous, so cutting, so sarcastic. You can positively hear the dead beauties saying, "Charles, I never know what you are *really* thinking," or "Charles, do smile, just once," or "Charles, dearest, why do you look at me like that? Have you forgotten. . . ." Heart-rending for them, but—also attractive, you know!

How many calculated storms must have beaten in vain tears against that stern rock of a face as he stood there, his Majesty the King, just waiting for the tempest to abate. It must have been one of the most useful expressions in history.

* * *

Waxworks ? Pooh !

That is what most visitors say as they trail round Westminster Abbey, wrestling painfully with the past, trying to flog their imaginations with dates.

How many realize that these waxworks were made by men who saw these kings and queens in life ? They are authentic portraits, less flattering perhaps than the works of greater artists, and for this reason more interesting. In fact, I prefer this waxwork of Charles II to Lely's splendid portrait. I am sure it is more like Charles.

From the time of Henry V till about 1700 every dead monarch was modelled in wax. This effigy was then dressed in the king's finest suit, and was carried through the streets of London in his funeral train. Westminster Abbey was once full of these marvellous relics—" The Ragged Regiment " they used to be called, or " The Play of Dead Folks." To-day only eleven are shown, the broken limbs of the others, the gruesome heads and hands, are locked away from public sight. Poor Edward I and Eleanor, the third Edward and Philippa, glorious Hal and Katharine, Henry VII and Elizabeth of York, James the First and Anne of Denmark, lie all jumbled together ; a sight that would have made Hamlet wince.

Was there ever a more pathetic puppet show ?

Kings and Queens

Enough remained of Queen Elizabeth for a clever restorer to give us a new idea of her. There she stands covered in jewels, holding her sceptre, her rich, red, velvet gown falling to a pair of surprisingly adequate brocade shoes. But this is not the imperious queen we know, this is not Gloriana, who could put on a Tower of London expression and whip men with her tongue. This is a sad old woman. She has uncanny, unhappy eyes ; such a lonely face.

William and Mary, who attract every Dutch visitor to London, are a heavy, homely couple. She wears purple velvet over a brocaded skirt, and he was so small that some thoughtful person mounted him on a footstool so that he might match his tall wife. Queen Anne is also on view, but she, too, is rather heavy and homely. Those are the royalties.

In a corner is Frances, Duchess of Richmond, who is said to have been the Britannia of the coinage. Just think of this ! Frances Teresa Stewart in wax looking across at a waxen Charles II ! What irony ! She, you remember, was the lady Pepys thought so lovely ; and he had a good eye. What scandal a wax figure can recall. " La Belle Stewart " never cared for chatter, however, and you can imagine how Charles looked when he learned that the beautiful scandalous creature, who might have been Queen of England, had eloped one night from Whitehall with the Duke of Richmond. It must have been a bad day for everybody in St. James's Palace. The cook, I should think, was certainly sacked.

The Heart of London

In the next case is Katherine, Duchess of Buckingham, who on her death-bed developed an enthusiasm for her funeral. She had previously arranged it in detail with the Garter King-of-Arms, and she lay there worrying if the trappings would be all right, and fearing to die before the undertakers sent the canopy for her approval.

" Why don't they send it," she cried, " even though all the tassels are not finished ? "

Poor lady ! Her pomp is ended, and her brocaded robes sadly in need of the dry-cleaner.

Nelson is there, modelled shortly after death, wearing his uniform, his neat, thin legs in white kerseymere breeches and silk stockings, and the Government " hat tax " stamp still to be seen inside his hat.

Full of human interest they are, but Charles is the gem. Time has been unkind to the fine point lace at his neck and at his wrists. It is almost black. His jaunty hat, with its drooping ostrich plumes, would disgrace a brawl ; yet I defy you to laugh at him. His Majesty looks at you from the dust of centuries, and you are inclined to hate the people who have written their names with diamonds on the plate glass, including the author of that famous quatrain which ends :

> He never said a foolish thing,
> Nor ever did a wise one.

Still he has an air with him, and when he entered

a room, his melancholy eyes burning in that sallow, set face, just think how the ostrich plumes swept the dust, and how the lovely naughtiness of his day curtseyed in gold brocade. . . .

Lost Heirs ✦ ✦ ✦ ✦ ✦

I WONDER how many people who live in London lodgings look in the mirror during their occasional shaves and think: "There goes the rightful Duke of Brixton!"

O the wild dreams of London! The old man who starves himself that he may search year after year for a document which conceals a coronet is only less tenacious than the elderly virgin whose sole passion is the belief that somebody way back in history "did her down" over a will. There are humble, ragged people who must be positively shocked when they cut a finger and discover that their blood is just ordinary red. There are others who believe themselves to be the ground-landlords of New York or Philadelphia, who go on living in the splendid hope that some day—some day—that missing document will turn up to smooth out the injustices of time.

The Record Office in Chancery Lane is the magnet which draws all these queer people year after year. These unofficial dukes and earls go off each morning with their luncheon in paper bags to hunt up their ancestors. They are all so certain. So convincing. You can put your head quite close to theirs and never hear the bee.

Their finger nails may be in mourning for their lost departed, their collars may be greyish, and their cuffs frayed, but they have butlers and scarlet carpets in their hearts, and in their eyes a

Lost Heirs

hunger most awful to see. There is a legend that one searcher who insisted on being called "my lord," became tired of trying to justify his claim and in a moment of enthusiasm hired a peer's robes and actually succeeded in entering the House of Lords during a State ceremony! What a moment!

There he stood for a moment among his peers. It must have been the greatest moment of his life. It was during the State opening of Parliament, and the House of Lords was waiting with lowered lights for that moment when the King and the Queen, with white-satined pages holding the royal trains, would enter at the precise moment, the lights leap up and send a green and fiery glitter rippling along the throats of the peeresses in the gallery. In this scene stood the peer from Bloomsbury or Brixton or Balham, watching with who knows what delicious thrills the Gentlemen-at-Arms standing at the doors holding their halberds in white gauntleted hands while the lights glanced off their golden helms. What a moment! And what, I wonder, betrayed him? Why did they ask him to go? Did he show too much confidence in his rightful surroundings, or did he say, "Granted, I'm sure," to the duke who trod on his foot? I wonder. . . .

When I entered the Record Office yesterday the curious round room, like the smoking-room of an Atlantic liner that has taken to book-collecting, was full of students and historians poring over spidery Elizabethan script or muttering the English of Chaucer's day beneath their breath.

The Heart of London

Now and again someone with the strawberry leaf complex wanders in here, puts an old hat on the chair, and calls for documents with the air of a rather weary Malvolio. Generally speaking, the legacy and title hunters gather next door in the Legal Search Room.

Here I found an assortment of women and men. Some were solicitors and barristers looking up records, some were trying to claim funds in Chancery, and others the usual fortune and title hunters.

This is merely a fraction of the interest this building holds for us. It houses twenty-six miles of shelves packed with historic documents and millions of unhistoric documents. Here are the bones of English History. Come into the Museum known so well to those who have a *flair* for the right things, the Americans. Here in two portly volumes is "Domesday Book," writ in a fair monkish hand. Shelves are stacked with letters from kings and queens, generals and admirals, cardinals and peers : humour, pathos, tragedy, passion. In one of these Wolsey, "the King's poore, hevy and wrechyd prest," asks Henry VIII to forgive him and take him back into favour. Queen Elizabeth's hand is set to a number of letters, and to her are missives from many men, including two who loved her. Robert Dudley, Earl of Leicester, says in one : "I humbly kiss your foot," and the imprisoned Earl of Essex is represented by a brief letter written for the eyes of Gloriana alone.

You can read letters which recall cannon shot

on the high seas, and letters which give a vision of deep political plotting and such-like villainy. " God has given us a good day in forcing the enemy so far to leeward," wrote Sir Francis Drake aboard the " Revenge." " I hope in God the Prince of Parma and the Duke of Sedonya shall not shake handes this fewe days." Quite near you will find the last confession of Guy Fawkes.

When you have enjoyed the flavour of these old days you may meet on the stairs an ordinary cat. At least so it seems. It is Felix, and he has been walking through history for centuries. It is the only cat officially on a Government staff—in spite of anything women secretaries in Whitehall may tell you ! It receives a penny a day from Government funds ! I believe that the terms of its appointment include a clause that it must keep itself clean, catch rats and mice, and bring up its children. If anybody killed the official cat in ancient times he had to forfeit sufficient wheat to cover the body.

* * *

The officer in charge of the Legal Search Room sits with the official list of lost money before him —the funds in Chancery, which, by the way, are only sufficient to make one decent full-blown millionaire—as millionaires go nowadays.

" Yes," he said, " there are some strange searchers.

" In the summer many good, democratic Americans come over to trace their ancestry back to William the Conqueror ! "

" And the lost heirs," I said—" the would-be dukes ? "

" Ah ! " he replied. " Ah ! "

He sighed.

I noticed a shabby old man mournfully shuffling out. I felt certain that there was the ghost of ermine over him, and I hope that now and then his landlady, just to keep his poor heart up, drops a curtsy when she brings in the kippers and says : " Dinner is served—*your grace.*"

Fish ∘ ∘ ∘ ∘ ∘ ∘ ∘

EVERY morning at the uncomfortable hour of five a man in a peaked cap rings a big bell in Billingsgate Market and the lights go up. Then the haddocks and plaice, which you eat in due course, begin their commercial career.

Shouting? Yes; most decidedly! The ozone which exudes from prostrate cod seems to have a singular effect on the lungs of the fish trade. In the old days, I am told, they used to shout definite fishy slogans such as: " Had-had-had-haddock ! " or " Wink-wink-wink-winkles ! " But only now and then, when some enthusiast becomes filled with the spirit of the past do you hear anything so interesting. It is mostly a swift, sharp, business-like affair, with a little violent auction-eering over in the corner. Lying in the Thames at the Wharf which is on one side of the market is a Danish trawler with North Sea salt caked on her funnel. Men run up and down the gangways carrying her cargo, while from every corner of the compass railway carts converge on that tangle of narrow streets which begins at the Monument. If you like statistics you will be interested to know that on an average eight hundred tons of fish pour into Billingsgate every day, and the majority comes by train.

I wandered between lines of dead fish. Nothing on earth can look so dead as a fish. It is, in a

lavish place of this kind, difficult to believe that
fish have ever lived, have ever sported gallantly
in the sea, making romantic love and building
homes, and generously seeing to it that we shall
go on having fish after soup.

Incredibly dead codfish and inconceivably
defunct skate lay strewn in rich profusion,
herrings with red eyes and white-bellied plaice—all
the fruit of the ocean mixed up with ice! Queer,
fascinating things are apparently weeded out
before they reach Billingsgate; there is none of
the strange, snarling fish you see at Boulogne or
Dieppe, none of the comic monstrosities with
green whiskers which enchant you in Marseilles.
Billingsgate is essentially an edible dump. Everything that comes into it is solemnly designed for
the kitchen.

Between the flabby corpses walk men and women
—fishmongers, hotel buyers, and the like—prodding, examining, comparing, now and then tasting
a shrimp—at five a.m., too!—sometimes cracking
an experimental mussel!

Officials of the Worshipful Company of Fishmongers patrol the place. They represent one
of the few old guilds which are still actively interested in the trades they represent. These
inspectors have the power to condemn anything
unfit for sale.

*　　　*　　　*

And the smell!
How many cats sniff it at the Bank, I wonder!
Smell is a marvellous thing. It can awaken the

Fish

most tender memories of love and passion, of moments under a red moon, blowing roses, blue nights. Were I a woman I would never allow the man I loved to go far without a bottle of my favourite scent. A photograph is a dead thing; a smell is alive. How strange, I thought, that Billingsgate should appeal to the same sense that thrills to a laced handkerchief. Here you have the harmony and discord of smell. Billingsgate in this musical metaphor is like a cat walking across a piano—worse, it is a blare of smell, an assault on the senses. I wondered if, with study, a keen nose could in time learn to disentangle the various strains that go to swell the mass effect, as a musician is able to deafen himself to a symphony and follow the steady hum of an individual 'cello. I was conscious, it is true, of the steady hum of haddock and a sharp piccolo-like movement from the plaice, but, apart from perhaps the steady drumming from the cod stalls, the finer, more subtle emanations escaped me, such as mullet.

Remembering a handkerchief I once had, so long ago that I can write of it as if it were a museum specimen, but in its time a marvellous thing that held within its creased folds all the nightingales of Monte Cattini, I asked myself this problem: Suppose a fishmonger had a passionate love-affair in Billingsgate, would fish remind him or would it not? At first I was inclined to say no, but on reflection I thought yes. He would meet the girl every day for months among the lobsters. He would see her come to him, so graceful and lissom, down an avenue of oysters. He would whisper to her above the whiting, and they would kiss among the crabs. Gradually turbot would come to have a deeper meaning for this man. He would hesitate over the whitebait, and—remember. When the first Danish herrings came in during February he would have to pull himself together and be strong. Years after, if he wished to sentimentalize, what simpler, or more poignant, than a quick sniff at a kipper ? But the agony of living in this hall of memories ! If you treasure a piece of scented cambric, just think how harrowing it would be to live in the perfume factory. . . .

Such speculation is vain. Do not pity Billingsgate. I hardly like to tell you because I fear you may not believe me, but——Billingsgate smells nothing ! No ; not even the faintest odour as of melons. Its nose is atrophied. I discovered this by the merest chance.

" By jove," I said, " that's a pretty loud fish. What is it ? "

" I don't smell anything," said the owner.

We discussed smell minutely, and I discovered that his life in Billingsgate had made him immune from fishy smells. How wonderful Nature is ! Only when he returns from his holiday is he conscious of a little something in the air.

* * *

Billingsgate is perhaps the most libelled spot in London. Fifty years ago you had to wax your ears. The language was awful. To-day the Billingsgate fish porters are as polite and charming as we all are.

Fish

They are the backbone of Billingsgate, for this market is worked on the most primitive system of hard transport. The Genoese galleys which in the Middle Ages anchored near by were unloaded in exactly the same way. So were Pharaoh's galleys, and Cæsar's. These men, wearing queer-shaped leather helmets rather like stunted Burmese pagodas, carry all the fish in crates on their heads. When a man's neck " sets," as they call it, he can carry sixteen stone on his head. They do it every day and all day.

" Mind your back, *please* ! " say the fish porters of Billingsgate.

" Shove over the hammer—if you don't mind, Jack ! " I heard one say.

" Certainly ! " replied Jack.

So much for that.

*　　*　　*

Then I walked out on Billingsgate Wharf and had a real thrill. This is where London began. It is probably the oldest wharf on the Thames. Old Geoffrey of Monmouth, who would have made a fine American reporter, says that it takes its name from Belin, King of the Britons four hundred years before Christ. Stowe thinks that it was once owned by a man called Biling. It is certain, however, that the Romans landed their furs and their wines here, and at this spot on the Thames the first imports of London were dumped, the first merchants gathered.

To the left I saw the bluish shadow of Tower Bridge. The brown Thames water licked the broad hull of a fish trawler. Crate after crate of herrings caught so far away in the North Sea were unloaded for London, and as I passed again through the ripe, rich tang of the market a man was buying lobsters which I suppose a lovely girl will enjoy as she makes eyes at someone over the rim of her champagne glass.

Haunted ✐ ✐ ✐ ✐ ✐ ✐

DEVONSHIRE HOUSE is dead and gone.
I hope that its name may be perpetuated
by the new commercial building, but I do not
know.

When the workmen were performing acute
surgical operations on old Devonshire House I
was interested to hear people, who knew the Duke
quite well by his photographs, express intimate
regret at this deed. "Dear old Devonshire
House!" they said. "What a shame it is that
these grand old. . . ." And so on and so forth.
They were wistful. They gave the impression
that they knew the pink bedroom awfully well
(don't you know) ; they that had lingered on
every inch of the famous staircase. They were
like people who mourned the downfall of the old
home.

You see, for nearly five years Devonshire House
was, in the name of charity, thrown open to the
public, so that probably more people were acquain-
ted with the geography of this mansion than with
any other ducal house which has not become either
an hotel or a museum. So :

"Poor old Devonshire House!"

"Yes, it looks just like a bombed château during
the war!"

*   *   *

It did.

The Heart of London

Workmen swarmed over it, stood on walls picking at it, sending it earthwards in clouds of dry, white dust. Great gashes had been cut in the sides, windows had been knocked out, the daylight shone into the out-buildings, exposing the discreet wall-paper of the servantry, and that wide-walled courtyard through which swung the coaches of Fox, Burke, and the "New Whigs" in the days when men, and many a pretty woman, plotted against Pitt, was the loading spot for builders' carts and a place in which anyone could light a bon-fire to burn lath and plaster.

There was great interest in this patch of changing London. Not one person passing on an omnibus but remarked about it; and no wonder, for this is Piccadilly's most dramatic assassination. In the sound of the picks you could hear the voice of the new age—or the Chancellor of the Exchequer, which ever you liked! These great houses round which centred the wit, the beauty, the scholarship, the politics, and the art of the eighteenth century have outlived their day. London has crept up from Ludgate Hill like a tidal wave and over-whelmed them.

Devonshire House stood, strange and incongruous behind its feudal wall, like the Lord Mayor's coach in a traffic hold-up. Great hotels and shops grew up and shouldered it, and still it stood there dreaming, it seemed, of a vanished paddock; aware, it seemed, in its gated caution, that once upon a time highwaymen rode out of Kensington with masks over their faces,

I admit that it was ugly—entirely gloomy in

its grey, stiff, barrack-like way; but it did mean
something—it had character. Though nobody, as
far as I am aware, ever did anything splendidly
bad or remarkably good in it, Devonshire House
could never be neutral. The National Anthem
is pretty bad music, but it could never be neutral!

* * *

So, as the workmen consumed their sandwiches
in halls through which for two centuries passed
a delicious trickle of royalties, as they heard the
whistle and rose heavily to grasp their picks and
do some more damage, I more than once stood
there among a tangle of builders' carts and saw
visions rise out of the white dust.

What a procession!

I saw the hackney coach of Charles James Fox
trundle under the portico. Burke, of course, was
there too, the practical, wise Burke; for here they
conspired with the Coalition Whigs to hit at Pitt,
whispering and plotting with the lovely Georgiana,
third Duchess of Devonshire, who enjoyed placing
her white finger into this political pie. There had
been a tea-party at Boston. And the French
Revolution was gathering like a storm to split
them. Among these crumbling stones Georgiana
must have heard of that scene, one of the most
dramatic the House of Commons has ever witnessed,
when these two, Fox and Burke, broke their
long friendship in a thrilled hush, Fox with tears
in his eyes and his voice breaking, Burke grim and
firm, and the House of Commons looking on at a
quarrel that never healed.

The Heart of London

George IV, as Prince of Wales, with his card-table fingers also in the Fox pie, and all the brains and elegance of that time, wits who have been forgotten, a few who live, laughter, music, and the flash of white shoulders, eyes above a fan. . . .

What a procession !

All this you could see in the dust of Devonshire House—two hundred years of it, duke succeeding duke ; and all the time the new generations of wealth, power, and art moving up to that grey old portico.

As I passed it late one night I wondered if there are spirits—a queer doubt to express to-day ! If so, I am certain that on calm nights fit for a lady's walk Georgiana, third Duchess of Devonshire, must have visited the ruin, looking with very straight brows and considerable " tut-tutting " at a big board on which was printed : " The magnificent building to be erected on this site will include offices, restaurants, and flats."

* * *

Poor Georgiana ! Time is a queer thing, and—you, in your time, would never have believed it, would you ?

About Homes in Bondage ✿ ✿ ✿

DO you wish to feel human emotion spring from inanimate things? Do you wish to meet ghosts? Then come with me to one of London's great furniture store-houses, in which a thousand homes lie piled to the roof, silent, sheeted, tomb-like.

A store-man switches on a line of lights, and we see stretching to the distance great pyramids of household goods, whole homes of furniture, neatly stacked and carefully ticketed against the time when a man and a woman will come to claim them. Some of the pyramids suggest Park Lane, others suggest Clapham Common.

Let us peep beneath this shroud, and what do we see: " Good morning, Mrs. Everyman, and what can I do for you? Kindly accept this cushion as a souvenir of your visit." There lies the gift cushion, there the once-so-loved instalment suite that was delivered in the plain van. Note the pictures by Watts, Rossetti, and others of the Victorians to whom the suburbs are so loyal. " Love's Awakening." Ah!

What do we see in the next tomb? Yes; here was an elegant home with a cheque-book behind it. The low satinwood dresser had a compartment like a knee desk, so that she might get close up when she rouged her lips, and three swinging mirrors in order that she might know whether her shoulders were evenly powdered

before he took her out to the Berkeley.
Engravings, a Japanese cabinet, a good one,
a beautiful round table with a surface like that
of a still pool. Little home and big home side by
side, social differences forgotten. Do you see the
ghosts of Mrs. Everyman and Lady Nobody
meeting like sisters over their shrouded homes
crying a little on each other's arms? I do. The
tombs go on waiting . . . waiting.

Homes in bondage!

As we wander down the line our eyes are caught
by a doll's house, relic of some distant nursery, a
child's cot, or a piece of furniture with distinct
personality, and we wonder how much heartache
and hope this place represents. There are people
living in lodgings dreaming of the home that they
will build again one day, longing to surround
themselves with loved things, to tear off the
wrappings and see again those precious ordinary
objects that mean so much in every life—those
sentimental anchors.

Sentiment—that is the keynote. Without it
London's store-rooms would be half empty.

"Yes, sir," says the store-man, as he pulls
aside a wrapping, "people don't seem able to
bring themselves to part with things. It's mighty
queer. Look at this old box, now—what would
you think is inside it?"

The box is an ancient nail-studded chest with
a curved lid that might have contained all the
gold of Treasure Island. I hazard a guess just
to please him.

"No, sir. It's just full of little old bits of cloth,

About Homes in Bondage

the kind of things that women collect and put in old baskets because they may come in useful some day. There's bits of tinsel and lace, and pretty little cases full of red and blue beads and needles by the score. But what's the sense of letting it eat its head off here? That's what I want to know. If they've paid a penny for this old box they must have paid fifty pounds, for it was here before ever I was. O yes, there's funny people about, and no mistake. Now if it belonged to me. . . .

As he rambles on, I examine the old box with interest. I know why it was put there; and so do you! Memories cling round it—memories so sweet that the heart revolts at the thought of burning those poor fragments.

Most people have a box of this sort. In it are queer trifles, little geometric nets on which beads are strung or sewn. Green and scarlet parrots preen themselves on half-finished trees. It is that note of half completion, as of a task suddenly put down and soon to be resumed, which makes such things so appealing. Perhaps a needle is still sticking in a corner of the fabric, waiting, it seems, for the fingers that will never come again. And when you look you see the hand that placed it there, you hear a voice and see a face bending over the pretty, unimportant thing, and it's ten to one that you are a child again on some slow, lazy afternoon of sun; and the voice is the voice of your mother telling you the same old story you have heard a hundred times as you watch her, fascinated by her brilliance, hypnotized by the growth of the brocade bird and its beaded eye : a masterpiece which fills your mind and stands out as the most marvellous and beautiful thing the world has ever seen. Clever, wonderful mother. . . .

" There's funny people about, and no mistake ! " says the storeman again, giving the box a prod with his foot.

We go on. He unties the wrappings round another deposit. All these things, he explains, belong to " a divorced couple." How new they are, he comments. How quickly they must have found out their mistake ; no sooner married than divorced and storing their things, and chucking away good money after bad !

I peep in with a feeling that I am eavesdropping. There, piled up sideways, is the table round which this unknown tragedy of married life was acted, the solemn, stiff chairs, witness to it all, the pictures which for a little while were gathered for this mockery of a home.

" Why they don't sell it I can't think," says the storeman.

I wonder, too, why they keep it ! Neither one nor the other can bear to live with it. Then what queer sentiment, what common memory, retains this split home here in the pathetic silence of lapsed things ?

We turn a corner. More avenues, sheeted, deserted.

" Some of these people are dead, we think," remarks my guide, waving his hand towards the dim roof. " This lot was put in at the beginning

About Homes in Bondage

of the war. We had to sell quite a lot. Payments lapsed, and no one replied to advertisements. It is a mystery to know who it belongs to now, sir, and that's a fact."

*   *   *

As we turn into another warehouse we meet a man and woman. They have pulled aside the sheeting and are standing among chairs and tables and pictures. The woman comes out and says nervously :

"We've just come to see our things. The manager said that we might."

As we enter the next compartment we hear this man and woman talking.

"Oh, look ! There it is, next to mother's writing-table. Do pick it up and let me hold it !"

There is the sound of the man walking over the stiff wrappings.

"Oh, my dear !" comes the woman's voice. "My dear !"

We go on through the silent aisles, the storeman talkative, amusing, insensible to the drama we have met, oblivious of the longing in those few words spoken by a woman, among the sheeted pathos of a home in bondage.

Royal Satin   *o o o o o*

WHEN the Queen was married she wore a dress which I find it rather difficult to describe, because there is a special dressmakers' language for this sort of thing.

It was low in the neck, the lowness draped with white lace. The tiny inch-long sleeves were caught up at the shoulder with little bunches of orange blossom. The corsage curved inwards to a tight waist ending in a point, and the dress, cut away over a fine white underskirt, fell in a graceful, generous sweep to the floor. Over the front were draped trailing sprays of orange blossom. The going-away dress is a bit easier to describe. It covered the Queen from neck to feet. The collar was high, and braided like that of a mess uniform or a commissionaire's tunic. The sleeves, tight at the wrist and braided, rose at the shoulder, sharply and alarmingly, in a queer shape, known, I believe, as " leg of mutton." It is very stately and ornate, and, in the light of modern fashion, exceedingly stiff and strange.

Men in the early 'thirties can just remember their mothers in a dress like this, sitting calm and lovely in a victoria with a parasol in their white-gloved hands, and a perky little hat like a vege-tarian restaurant poised on their puffed-up hair. So you can't help loving the Queen's going-away dress. . . .

*   *   *

Royal Satin

Where can you see it? Do you know? It is on view with hundreds of other royal satins in that beautiful and comparatively unknown museum within a stone's throw of the Prince of Wales's house in St. James' Palace—the London Museum. This is a woman's museum. I cannot imagine a woman who would not be thrilled by it. In the first place, it is the most beautifully housed museum in the world. Lancaster House, which used to be the town house of the Dukes of Sutherland, is one of the finest houses in London. It makes you feel good all over simply to walk up the wide, dignified staircase that leads from the great marble entrance hall. In the second place, the London Museum contains rooms filled entirely with royal treasures: dolls dressed by Queen Victoria, a tiny suit worn by King Edward, the cradle in which the present Royal Family were rocked to sleep, the coronation robes, intimate family relics that recall Queen Victoria, the Prince Consort, and King Edward. There are also beautiful, slightly-faded dresses which Queen Alexandra wore when she came over the sea many years ago to be the Princess of Wales.

*   *   *

Every day a few women can be found in a state of ecstasy before these cases. Sometimes the keeper, frock-coated and white-spatted and gardeniaed, can be seen conducting a tall, stately woman through the high magnificence of the halls —a woman who looks with a smile at many a relic of childhood; and people whisper " The Queen! "

The Heart of London

To the Londoner this place holds more of interest than any other museum, not excepting the unfortunately entombed Guildhall Museum.

The whole history of London, dug up out of London clay and peat, is here for inspection. The finest collection of Roman pottery, found among the roofs of London, is on view. There is a pot which dates from perhaps A.D. 200, on which a Londoner of seventeen hundred years ago has written : " Londini ad fanum Isidis " (" London, next door to the Temple of Isis "). Think of it ! In Tudor Street seventeen hundred years ago men worshipped the Egyptian goddess Isis, the goddess with the moon on her head, the sister-wife of Osiris, who travelled from the Nile to the Tiber, where she joined the impartial Pantheon of Rome !

There is the skeleton of a Roman galley found in the bed of the Thames : a great ship in which men came to build the first London. There is the skeleton of one of the first Londoners, lying stretched under glass as he was found, with a bronze pin under his chin and a bronze dagger at his breast bone.

Down below in the basement is a Chamber of Horrors few people know. Here are the great iron gates of Newgate Prison. Here in a frightening gloom are two prison cells. A wax figure, who looks as if the execution morning has dawned, writhes on his hard bed, his hands chained to the walls. Here are the manacles that held Jack Sheppard.

In another room are a series of lifelike models of old London which every Londoner should see

Royal Satin

and admire. Old London Bridge, with its rows of traitors' heads set on staves, is lifelike; old St. Paul's during the Fire of London is wonderful. A mechanical contrivance gives the illusion that smoke is rolling up from the blazing church over the startled city, the windows of houses show blood-red lights, and, as you stand looking at the model, your imagination is stirred so that you can hear the cries and the shouting, see the confused rushes as citizens tried to save their treasures when liquid lead was falling in a hissing stream on the red-hot pavements round St. Paul's.

*   *   *

One wonders what Lancaster House will be like in fifty years' time if it keeps pace with London! Already a hansom cab is parked in the garden! Some day a motor-omnibus and perhaps a tramcar will arrive. There are crowded days ahead!

Among the Fur Men ✦ ✦ ✦ ✦

WOMEN must, I am glad to say, have fur coats. It has been so since we men set out after the ermine with clubs instead of cheque books, and splendidly have they always repaid us with a glimpse of eyes over soft fur and chins buried in the cosy rightness of it.

The result is that, all over the world, wherever hairy things creep, crawl, or climb, men are ready with guns and traps. Three times a year the pelts of the world pour into London to be distributed. Whenever this happens a large auction-room in Queen Street will provide you with the strangest sight in the City of London. You walk in through a courtyard past a man in white overalls. As I passed him recently he said : " Hudson Bay Company selling now, sir ! " and, do you know, I felt young all over ! I thrilled. Hudson Bay Company ! Shades of Fenimore Cooper ! In one swift, pregnant moment I saw the white lands I used to know so well when I was at school, the driving sheets of snow, the tugging sleigh dogs, and the big, square-bearded men, with matted hair frozen under round fur hats, bending forward against the storm, urging on their teams, taking their piled sleighs to the trading post.

I crossed the courtyard and entered the auction-room. What a scene ! Men who buy furs in every country in the world were present. They sat tier on tier, a good five hundred of them,

Among the Fur Men

looking like a full session of the Parliament of the United States of Europe. No common auction this: it was a fur parliament, a senate of seal and musquash. Russians, Poles, Germans, Dutch, French, every kind of Jew, and a good balance of English and American. If Sir Arthur Keith had been with me he would have gone crazy over the marvellous skulls and cheek bones. It was, anthropologically, a splendid sight.

They retained their hats as they sat in the wide half-moon of the fur theatre. What hats! Here and there I picked out a round astrakhan cap, and, of course, there were fur coats. One man unbuttoned his coat. Somebody had been killing leopards!

Seven men sat high up above the assembly, facing it, and in the centre of the seven was the auctioneer:

" Any advance on three hundred ? "

Instead of the nods and lifted eyebrows of any ordinary saleroom there was a violent agitation. To make a bid in this room a man had to create a scene. In two minutes the place looked like a crisis in the French Senate. Men desiring mink rose and shot up their arms. The three hundred pounds advanced to five hundred, hesitated, and spurted on to seven hundred. Then a man with a Central European beard rose (exposing a fine nutria lining) and carried the day. The hammer fell! At least twenty more women would have fur coats next winter!

*　　*　　*

The Heart of London

So it went on. Millions of potential fur coats were bought and—not one of them in sight! They were all lying in warehouses somewhere in London; they had all been carefully examined before the sale.

As it proceeded it occurred to me how true it is that certain professions take hold of a man and brand him. There are grooms who look like horses, dog fanciers who resemble dogs, and if certain of these fur men had emerged from thick undergrowth nine sportsmen out of ten would have taken a pot shot at them. I fancied I could detect the little rodent-like beaver merchants, the fat, swarthy seal fans, the sharp, pale-white fox-fanciers, and a few aristocratic grey men with whom I associated chinchilla.

*　　*　　*

The story behind it all! That was the thing that thrilled me. Behind this roomful of strange, intent men in a London auction-room I seemed to see other men, the wild, uncouth men of youthful romance, out in the savage places of the earth and in the great loneliness of forests and ice. Hunters, trappers! Though we grow old and hard and inaccessible to all soft thoughts we will never lose our love for these. It is in our blood. We have all longed to be trappers, we have all longed to blaze the trail through the Canadian wilderness, to crack the ice on Great Whale River before we could catch our breakfast, to win home at last in a flurry of snow to the log cabin. . . .

Among the Fur Men

" Any advance on three hundred and fifty pounds ? "

The baying of dogs in a white-sheeted world, the pine trees in shrouds ; and then—silence. . .

" Four hundred.   Any advance ? "

The green glitter of ice and the drama of a man fighting the elements, fighting solitude, primitive, uncouth, his mind following the minds of beasts as a fox-hunter anticipates the mind of a fox.

" Five hundred !   Any advance ? "

Blood over the snow and a limp body, the cracking of whips, the dog team with its laden sledge, and—all in order that you, my dear, may wrap your tall, elegant self in a lovely fur coat !

" Going, going, gone ! "

Crack !

Appeal to Cæsar   ✿   ✿   ✿   ✿

IN a high room overlooking Downing Street
sit six solemn men at a table piled with
books.

I recognize Lord X. and Lord Y. and Lord Z.
diligently reading, saying " Ha ! " or " Hum ! "
or looking grave, or reflectively wiping the lenses
of their spectacles. Two attendants in evening
dress, like a couple of lost waiters, tip-toe round
the apartment pulling out more books from the
well-stocked walls to place before their omniverous
lordships. The room is carpeted with maroon
felt, a few portraits in oils gaze down on the
assembly with polite indifference ; and there are
four fire-places set in squares of veined marble.
The furnishings resemble those of ideal offices in
the " efficiency first " advertisements : the inkpots are bigger and more efficient-looking than
ordinary inkpots, the desks are more prairie-like
in size than common desks, and the chairs more
comfortable than less exalted chairs.

Yes ; but what is happening ? I would think
if I did not know that a millionaire's will was
being read in a country house library. A few
barristers in wigs and gowns sit quietly reading as
if they were in chambers. Facing the peers is a
barrister standing at a little reading-desk, and in
the comfortable hush his crisp voice goes on and
on. An attendant discreetly feeds one of the four
fires, pokes a second, looks critically at a third ;

one of the peers calls for yet another book . . .
the Voice goes on and on and on. . . .

This is the highest court in the British Empire.
Behind that door in the corner is, theoretically,
the King. The Voice that goes on and on is
speaking on the steps of the throne. This is a
sitting of the Judicial Committee of the Privy
Council.

Whenever that old cry, " I appeal to Cæsar ! "
goes up in any part of the Empire this room
becomes busy. In this room the last word is
given on legal differences throughout the Empire.
If the courts in Australia cannot satisfy someone
about his right-of-way the trouble is smoothed
out once and for all here in Downing Street. If
there is a row in Canada about mining rights, in
New Zealand about water supply, in India about
delicate matters of caste, or even—as in a case
coming on soon—about a contract for the supply
of ground nuts, the Privy Councillors hear it on
behalf of the King and give their final and irre-
vocable verdict.

This room is the final appeal for four hundred
million British subjects, or nearly a third of the
human race. Legal controversies over eleven
million square miles—and strangely, throughout
the Church in this country—are settled here. Its
decisions go to the uttermost ends of the earth.
No court in the world has ever had so wide a
jurisdiction.

When I walked in, the two attendants looked up
curiously at me, for a strange face is a novelty.
The highest court in the Empire, although it is as

public as the Law Courts, seldom attracts a visitor.

I sit down in a kind of superior pew. Behind me are shelved the legal records of Canada, a library in themselves. " Revised Statutes of Nova Scotia," I read. " Quebec Revised Statutes," " New Brunswick Acts," " Laws of P. E. Island," " Revised Statutes of Alberta," and so on—the ideal bedside library ! " Canada," however, is not the official title : the Dominion laws are catchlined " North America."

Opposite are the laws of India, Australia ; and so on throughout the Empire.

* * *

What do litigants in distant parts of the earth think of this room ? Surely they imagine the King's Privy Council sitting robed as peers in the neighbourhood of a stained glass window, trailing ermine sleeves over richly carved chairs, light falling on coronets, with perhaps the King, in full Garter robes, dropping in to see how things are going on !

Nothing of the kind ! The highest court in the Empire sits in less state than a police court. There is no jury and no impassioned Law Court rhetoric. Counsel leans over his little reading-desk and talks to their lordships in a quiet, conversational voice. It is more like a directors' meeting than an Empire's appeal court. I half expect someone to rise and declare a dividend !

" And now," says the Voice in the quiet tone of a secretary reading an annual report, " I would

Appeal to Cæsar

like your lordships to look at page four hundred and two."

Their lordships comply.

What strange things go on here! One day they discuss an obscure passage in the Koran, the next they are debating the inner meaning of the Hedaya. When they deal with South Africa's Roman-Dutch law they bandy the names of Grotius and Vinnius, authorities the Law Courts never hear!

Stranger things than this happen. Did you know that in parts of the British Empire the old French law, long expelled from France, lives on, regulating men's lives. Appeals from Mauritius and the Seychelles Islands refer to the Code Napoleon! When Quebec submits its troubles to London this room hears, like an echo from long ago, mention of the ancient Custom of Paris; and the two men in evening dress go tip-toeing round the room to look over the shelves for Beaumanoir and Dumoulin!

Just think of that!

•   •   •

As I creep away from the Privy Council, feeling that it is one of the most wonderful places in London, that Voice goes on and on, quiet, conversational, and—the echo will be heard in Bombay!

Tons of Money ✍ ✍ ✍ ✍ ✍

THERE is no mystery about the making of money. The Royal Mint is exactly like any other factory. This surprised me. I felt that the manufacture of money must surely be surrounded by the unusual. It hardly seemed natural that this metal for whose possession we sweat and slave, lie and slander, and even, on occasions, commit murder, should be churned out by nonchalant machines no different in their general attitude towards production from those machines which cut out nails or stamp out dust bins.

It was with quite a shock that I watched a half-crown machine at work. What an ideal birthday present! The thing hypnotized me. Click-click-click-click it went, and at every click a silver-white half-crown was born, a real good half-crown ready to be spent. What a generous mouth the machine had ; how casual it was. . . .

" Click-click " went the metal millionaire, shooting its lovely children into a rough wooden trough. The pile grew as I watched it. It began with a taxicab fare ; the next second a twin was born ; they lay together for a second before they represented a solicitor's fee, or a dog licence ; in five more seconds there was a whole pound lying there. So it went on hour after hour while spectators stood by reverently feeling that the machine was grinning as it pounded away enthusiastically producing potential ermine cloaks, motor-cars, freehold houses, and winters in the south of France.

If only the Chancellor of the Exchequer would lend it to me for a week!

* * *

How much easier money is to make than to earn!

The first stage in the life of a half-crown is a hot foundry where men melt down bars of silver in crucibles. These crucibles lie in gas furnaces that roar like hungry lions and give out a beautiful orange flame ending in a fringe of apple-green light.

An overhead crane runs along, picks a red-hot crucible from the furnace, and carries it to a place where a series of long moulds are waiting. The silver is poured, spluttering and blazing, into these moulds, and the result is a number of long, narrow silver bars, which are passed through runners till the five-foot strip of silver is the exact thinness of a half-crown.

These strips are then passed through machines which punch out silver discs with remarkable speed. The next machine gives these plain silver discs a raised edge, and the next—the machine worth having—puts the King's head on them, mills their edges, and turns them out into the world to tempt mankind.

* * *

While I was in the stamping-room of the Mint all the machines were working full blast, except one which looked like a rich relation and had

The Heart of London

become muscle bound. In one corner they were making East African shillings by the hundred thousand, in another they were turning out West African currency. The men had as much as they could do to keep pace with them. No sooner had they carried away a trough full of money, with the blasé air such an occupation induces, than a second pile was lying there on the floor like a miser's hoard.

I saw enough African money made in half an hour to buy elephants, thousands of wives, guns, horses, buffaloes, and a throne or two.

The raw material of a sultanate fell out on the floor of the Mint before luncheon-time.

I could not, however, get worked up on African money. My first bucketful of sixpences gave me a much greater thrill. There must have been at least three thousand of them lying in bran. In the shilling department they were turning out a good line in high-class shillings, and the half-crown corner became positively thrilling.

" Where's the gold ? " I said, feeling slightly heady.

" Ah, where ? " replied my guide.

" America ? " I suggested.

" Ah—um," he said reflectively.

Leading from the stamping-rooms are rooms where silver is polished, but more interesting is the room in which its sound is tested. I have often heard money talk, but I had never heard it sing before. How it sings !

Men sit at little tables picking up half-crowns and dashing them against a steel boss, with the result that the air is full of something quite like bird song ; only much more interesting. It would surprise you to see how slight a defect disqualifies a coin. The smallest irregularity in its ring, and, flip ! it is lying in the " rejected " basket.

I half hoped they allowed staff and visitors to have these throw-outs at bargain prices ; but there was nothing doing.

* * *

In other rooms men crouched over a revolving hand covered with money, picking out any badly coloured coin as the constant stream advanced towards them. The next department was a mechanical weighing-room, in which wise-looking machines in glass cases put true coins in one slot, light ones in a second, and heavy-weights in a third.

As a climax I saw a giant machine that counts half-crowns into one hundred pound bags and never makes a mistake. I watched it count forty bagsful and then walked thoughtfully away.

* * *

" What does it feel like to make money all day long and draw a few pounds on Friday ? " I asked a Mint worker.

" Oh, I dunno," he replied as he shook a thousand pounds through a bran sieve.

This is a merciful frame of mind.

Where Time Stands Still ❧ ❧ ❧

LONDON is full of antique shops—places where Chinese Buddhas gaze pointedly at the alleged work of Chippendale—but if you asked me which is the most remarkable of all I would take you to a shop which deals only in articles more than a thousand years old.

When you enter, the centuries drop away like sand in an hour-glass. Through the frosted opacity of the door you are dimly aware of the red blur of a passing omnibus, of shadows that are men and women busying about their day's work. You hear the sound that is London ; but it means nothing in here. How can it ? It is a fluid unimportance called To-day and you are surrounded by Yesterday. The Present and the Future are intangible things. The Past only can be grasped and loved. That, at least, is how they think in this queer shop where Time is regarded as a mere convention ; a shoreless ocean in which each man's life is just a spoonful taken and returned.

The men who wander in look mostly dull and dry, sunk in whiskers and absent-mindedness. They sometimes leave their umbrellas in the rack and say " yes " when they should have said " no." They often remark on the wonderful weather when it is pouring with rain. They are probably thinking, you see, of some Grecian dawn or the raising of the siege of Troy. When you

know them, and can pull them out of the Past a
little, you realize that there is nothing more human
on earth than the average archæologist, because
he has learned that human men and women have
always been much the same, and that a little
thing like two thousand years and a pair of spats
makes no real difference to human nature, its
passions, its frailties, and its frequent glories. In
their packed minds Thebes, Athens, Rome, London,
Paris, and New York, march shoulder to shoulder
with nothing to distinguish them, except, perhaps,
a red omnibus going to Victoria.

It is so delightful to hear them talk about
Jason as if he threw up work in Threadneedle
Street to go out to Australia in search of fleeces ;
and once an old man told me about the marriage
of his grand-daughter with such remote charm
that it was three days before I realized that he
had not been talking about Cupid and Psyche.

* * *

However, let us glance round this shop. The
first impression is that some tidal wave of Time
has swept into it all kinds of articles caught up
in the ruin of the ancient world of Egypt, Greece,
Rome—these three great early civilizations are
the chief contributors, though, of course, Assyria
and Babylon are represented too.

Nearly everything you see has come from a
tomb. There are hundreds of thousands of objects
from the tombs of ancient Egypt. There is blue,
green, and gold glass from tombs in Cyprus ; there
is amazing coloured glass blown by Phœnicians at

the time of the Exodus, and—to come down to
quite modern times—there are lamps which lit
the ancient Romans to bed a thousand years ago,
and Greek vases with shaggy, horned satyrs
leaping round them after flying nymphs.

There are bronzes green with age, bright gold
which never loses its colour no matter how old it
is, shining glazed pottery which looks as if it had
come yesterday from Staffordshire, save for the
fact that it is finer than modern pottery and
contains a rough scratched cross and the words in
Latin : " Caius, his plate."

*　　*　　*

What is the charm of it ? What chains these
men to the past, archæologist and collector ?
Most of them are poor, for there is no money in it,
and most of them are intensely happy.

Just see the way they finger a bronze that was
cast when St. Paul was bearing the message of
Christianity through the world. There is perhaps
one part æstheticism in their love and one part
association. For them an object is not only full
of beauty but also full of magic ; it is like a
talisman that has the power to call up visions.
I have no doubt that when these old men hold
their treasures they can see the hosts of Pharaoh
sweeping through Syria, the nodding of the plumes,
the drive of arrows and all the confusion of an
ancient war. They can recreate round a relic a
dead empire. They feel that they possess something of the mighty personality of old times just
as in millions of lives a treasured letter can call

up " the touch of a vanished hand and the sound of a voice that is still."

In these old things the Past lives again ; they release the perfume of old loves, the violence of old ambitions, the thunder of marching troops, and the sailing of galleys over a morning world.

* * *

So if you collide violently with an old man who is carefully holding a little paper parcel, do not blame him for not seeing you !

You ! Good Lord—*you* !

My Lady's Dress ✎ ✎ ✎ ✎

MADAME requires a gown. In a building
high up above a celebrated street in the
heart of London, M. Flair bows her to a gold couch
on which are green velvet cushions.

M. Flair has descended with dignity and charm
to middle age, and every one seems to forgive him
for smelling rather like an overworked jasmine
grove. This apartment with the gold and black
striped cushions, the dove-grey walls, the black
carpet, the green jade hangings, and its scent like
that of Paris is not a shop : it is a *salon*. If you
pulled out a bunch of crackling fivers and offered
in an honest straightforward way to pay M. Flair
for one of his gowns—I mean " creations "—he
would, I imagine, feel insulted. He would much
rather sue you in the usual way. He is an artist.
Lady So-and-So blazons his genius along the Côte
d'Azur ; Miss So-and-So does him credit on the
stage, so that, as he bends over Madame, cooing
slightly, the tips of his manicured fingers together,
there is no condescension in him. Oh, dear, no !
He is a psychologist.

*　　　*　　　*

Madame requires a gown.

It must, I fear, be said that Madame has been
requiring gowns for well over forty years, and,
lately, requiring them shorter in the skirt, with an
ever-increasing touch of springtime over them.

My Lady's Dress

So M. Flair, after lightly discussing the season in the south of France and dismissing Switzerland with a shrug, whispers a word to a sylph in black and—more bowing—offers Madame a small brown Russian cigarette.

*　　*　　*

"Charming! delicious . . . ah, exquisite!"

These words come lightly from Madame as the grey curtains part at the end of the room, and there dawn, swaying slightly, hands on narrow hips, several visions of beauty clothed, it seems, too perfectly from their neat, sharp shoes to their tight little hats.

One mannequin is fair, another is dark, a third is petite, a fourth is tall. Each one is the perfection of her type—too perfect. As each sways up to Madame over the black carpet she gives Madame one half-smiling look in the eyes, then turns, lingers, sways a little, and slowly goes. Sometimes Madame puts out a hand and touches a gown. The mannequin stands like a piece of machinery suddenly stopped. All the time M. Flair remains with one plump hand on the gold couch, explaining, expounding, and, at length, advising. Here we have thin ice. Dangerous ice. M. Flair knows Madame's age and the lines of her figure. Madame has forgotten the first and has never really appreciated the second. This is where M. Flair earns his money. Just as he is bringing her—oh, so cleverly—away from a May-time gown to one nearer August, the curtains part, and into the scented room glides a Golden Girl—sweet as April sun.

Ah, now we approach the comedy; now the plot thickens; now Madame permits the white ash of her slim brown cigarette to fall unnoticed on the black floor. That splendid, cunning fall of the cloth, revealing that which it professes to cover; that fine swing of rounded hips; those beautiful young arms, unmasked at the elbow with no wicked little wizened witch's face time puts there. Yes; a lovely gown! Madame looks at April and—sees herself!

M. Flair knows that the game is up. He realizes, with the instinct of a lifetime's experience, that no matter what he can say Madame will have nothing but the unsuitable magnificence worn by this most marvellous of mannequins. The artist in him wars with the business man. He feels that he should forbid it. Refuse to sell. Explain to Madame that she will not look like the Golden Girl; that she is deluding herself. Yet why?

Madame, with a woman's swift knowledge of unspoken things, says:

" So you think it's a bit too—too young ? "

She appears frank, careless; but there is such a touch of hardiness in her voice, velvet over steel. It is a challenge to M. Flair to say " Yes," and what man would have the moral courage ?

" My dear lady," he says with uplifted hands. " What a ridiculous idea ! "

Then, when she has gone, he says to me: " You see how it is—O mon Dieu ! "

* * *

My Lady's Dress

" Yes, but the Golden Girl," I say. " How did anything so beautiful happen in the world ? The racehorse lines of her, the slimness, the strength. Is she one of these exiled princesses ? She must stand on a pyramid of good breeding."

" Oh, no," replies M. Flair ; " her father was, I believe, a coal-porter somewhere in London. If only her accent were a little better she might . . . the stage . . . success . . . but—O *mon Dieu*, these women who do not know themselves ! "

So ends an ordinary little comedy of a London day.

St. Antholin's ❧ ❧ ❧ ❧ ❧

I WENT into a City church the other day to hear a sermon that has been going on for three hundred and twenty years!

St. Mary Aldermary (not Aldermanbury) is an attractive Wren church tucked away on the north side of Queen Victoria Street. When I entered I found about forty middle-aged men and twelve women. They were sitting dotted about the church listening to a clergyman who was leaning earnestly over the pulpit talking about sin, the devil, and St. Paul. It was luncheon-hour in the City. It was also raining with ghastly persistence, and I thought at first that this congregation of fifty numbered many who might have sought refuge from the weather. A second glance assured me that this was an unworthy thought; here was an audience of devout, middle-aged City men with every mark on them of regular attendance. The rows of bald or grizzled heads were inclined towards the speaker, every word was followed with deep interest, save in one corner, where a little old man in a frock coat appeared to slumber.

" And what does St. Paul say. . . ."

The voice echoed round the church, and I smiled to think that I was listening to one of the longest sermons on record—a sermon that has been in progress for three hundred and twenty years! It happened like this.

*   *   *

St. Antholin's

There was once an ancient church in Watling Street called St. Anthonie's or vulgarly, St. Antholin's. It must have been an interesting church. It was full in its later period of Presbyterian fire and fury. It was also full of epitaphs, one of which I cannot resist quoting. It covered the bones of Sir Thomas Knowles, Mayor of London about 1399 :

> *Here lyeth graven under this stone*
> *Thomas Knowles, both flesh and bone,*
> *Grocer and alderman, years forty,*
> *Sheriff and twice mayor, truly ;*
> *And for he should not lye alone,*
> *Here lyeth with him his good wife Joan.*
> *They were together sixty year,*
> *And nineteen children they had in feere.*

Two hundred years after this remarkable epitaph, St. Antholin's became notorious as the head-quarters of the Puritan clergy. The bell used to ring at unearthly hours of the morning, and all the High Churchmen in Cheapside turned uneasily in their beds and perhaps politely gnashed their teeth. In 1599 a group of citizens founded a lectureship. They gave certain property in London which was to pay for a daily lecture in the pulpit of St. Antholin's. The church became famous as a lecture theatre. Lilly, the astrologer, used to go there. Scott makes Mike Lambourne refer to it in " Kenilworth."

The great fire burned down the church but still the daily lecture went on ; it was rebuilt and the lecture was continued in the new St. Antholin's; it was demolished in 1870, and the lecture was transferred to St. Mary Aldermary, where I heard it yesterday!

The sermon ended. The congregation rose. The little old man in the frock coat, who I imagined was deep in sleep, sprang to his feet and boomed " Amen ! "

" I've been here twenty-five years," said a verger, " and most of the people you see here are regular attendants. That old man in a frock coat was here when I came."

* * *

In a solicitor's office in Cannon Street I picked up the strings of a romance that has been acted time and again in London. The property bought in 1599 went on increasing in value, the St. Antholin lecture increased from one a week to two a week. Still the property increased in value, and funds accumulated till it was necessary to have a sermon every day, except Saturday.

" The conditions on which the lectures are to be delivered are all set down in the old deeds," said one of the solicitors who administers the lectureship. " The clergyman who preaches must be a rector in charge of 2,000 souls, must not live more than seven miles as the crow flies from the Mansion House, and must not have a stipend of over £300."

Some of the clergy who took up this three hundred and twenty year old sermon and carried it on for a while now wear bishop's gaiters.

St. Antholin's

So in the calm of these days the Puritanical fury of three hundred and twenty years ago, filtered through three centuries, goes on and on and on in the City of London! If the worthy old citizens came back from the Shades they would not be able to find their old church, but the Voice they subsidized still speaks, and the property they left . . . well, they would have the shock of their lives!

Not for Women ✿ ✿ ✿ ✿

THE place is generally blue with smoke and it smells strongly of grilled chops.

It is full of men : men eating and talking. Some do not remove their overcoats or hats, although the rooms are uncomfortably warm. This spot is remarkable only for the fact that it is one of the last eating-houses in London which does not cater for or encourage women. Sometimes a woman finds her way in, and all the men look up curiously, as early Victorians might have done to see a lone woman in a chop-house. They blink at her. They watch her covertly as she eats, not impudently, but with a slight pity, for she is, poor thing, unwittingly transgressing an unwritten law. She has no right to be there ! Generations of males have marked this place out as a feeding-place, and the funny thing is that no matter how you admire women generally, and adore some individually, you feel unhappy when you see one there. You want to put a screen round her and forget her. She is all wrong there. It is like going to your tailors and finding a pretty girl being measured for a costume. It surprises and unsettles your conception of the fitness of things !

Through the smoke and the stimulating smell— which I believe is a kind of barrage put up against the feminine—move women and girls of a type quite different from the usual waitress. They resemble more the handmaids of inns in, say, the time of Sterne. They have a sharp, ready way with them, and they regard the zoo of hungry men dependent on them with the faint superiority of the ministering female. They treat elderly barristers who inquire testily for an overdue sausage rather like a school matron reproving a greedy boy.

How efficient they are ! They blow down a tube and order all at once a sole, two grilled sausages, liver and bacon, a chop and apple tart, and never do they make a mistake in their destinations.

At first sight you might think that everybody comes here because it is cheap. A second glance shows you a curious assortment. There are celebrated barristers—the Lord Chief Justice often used to go there when he was Attorney-General—solicitors, journalists, at least one solemn editor of a literary monthly, and a floating population of publishers' readers, poets, authors, and others with business in the Street of Misadventure.

On your left two barristers discuss a case, on your right two newspaper men whisper all the things not yet printed in a murder or conspiracy trial, and in the corner two or three men who have not lost their undergraduate voices argue about an unpublished novel.

" Of course, the residuary legatee is in exactly the same position as that in Rex *v*. Tolbooth, and I therefore think you will agree. . . ."

This from the left. From the right :

" The police know perfectly well who did it,

but they daren't say so—yet. Of course, you've heard . . ." And from the corner:

" You can't do it with your tongue in your cheek ! You must be sincere ! You must believe in it, no matter how bad it is. Have you read——"

Then, slowly, peevishly, comes the inevitable Dickensian, the old man whose collars and neck-ties seem deathless, whose clothes have a queer cut, whose hat, while it does not actually challenge modernity, does not conform to any current mode. He is angry. Some young upstart is sitting at *his* table, the table at which he has probably eaten about fifteen thousand chops. Ancient kings must have looked like this when they caught a virile baron trying on the crown ! Insolence and— worse ! Much worse. An awful reminder to a man of habit ! Some day . . . ah, well, that day has not come, and till it does he will sit at that particular table and eat his chop with his particular knife and fork. So he stands about glowering and fidgeting, the bland young man calmly eating, an innocent usurper.

But the clash between man and man is as nothing compared with the drama of a woman's entrance. Most women reach the door and instinctively realize that they have blundered into man's last stronghold and beat a tactful retreat, coughing slightly. Now and again some insensi-tive or ignorant man actually brings a poor woman there. Sex consciousness is a queer thing. Go into a telephone exchange where you are the only man and see how you like it. These women who suddenly dawn like a crime in the unwritten convention of this place must feel it too ; but women are so accustomed to scrutiny.

Is it fancy or does an uneasy silence pass like a cloud over the babel of law, newspaper, and book talk ?   I wonder.

Anyhow, it is remarkable to find any place in London in which woman is an anachronism, and no doubt the day is coming when they will storm even this barricade and—then we may have more comfortable chairs and nicer tables and a change in wall-paper !

Our Roman Bath ✦   ✦   ✦   ✦

AN American once told me in Vienna that the Strand possesses a Roman bath well worth seeing, but, being a perfectly good Londoner, I did not believe him—till I went there.

This bath, which was constructed in A.D. 200—seventeen hundred and twenty-five years ago—is exactly opposite Bush House, in the Strand! Think of it! Bush House and Rome! It is in the basement of No. 5, Strand Lane, an astonishing, narrow, dingy alley that in one step takes you back to the darkest days of Victorian London, when lanterns glimmered in passages and "Peelers" twirled truncheons and wore stovepipe hats. No. 5 belongs to the Rev. Pennington Bickford, Rector of St. Clement Danes, who bought the house three years ago to save the bath, which was—O incredible London!—in danger of destruction.

After writing my name in a school exercise book, which contains addresses in China, Japan, America, Canada, Australia (but few in London), I was taken by an intelligent young man into a high-vaulted place of red brick. What a splendid bath! How different from the bath-rooms of modern London, which are tucked away in houses like afterthoughts. Even a rich man I know, who has ten bath-rooms in his house, has no bath as fine as this. It is, of course, sunk in the floor. It is fifteen feet six inches in length by six feet nine inches—a proper lovable, wallowable bath, built by the only nation that understood baths and bathing.

It is an apse-headed oblong in shape, and I have seen exactly the same thing in the Roman ruins of Timgad, among the mountains of North Africa. No doubt it belonged to some rich Roman who built his villa seventeen hundred years ago some little distance from busy London, so that his wife and children might enjoy the flowers of the Strand, the peace, and the river.

The young custodian took a long-handled ladle and dipped it into the clear, limpid water which for seventeen centuries has been trickling into the bath ! It comes from an unknown spring bubbling from a " fault " in the London clay.

" You'd be surprised at the visitors, mostly Canadians and Americans, who want to take off their clothes and plunge in," said the guide, " not because it's a Roman bath, but because Dickens used to bathe here, and mentions it in Chapter thirty-five of ' David Copperfield.' "

" And do you ever let them ? "

" Not likely ! When I tell them how cold it is they change their minds. It's always three degrees above freezing."

" How do you know ? "

" Because I fell in once," he replied simply.

*   *   *

I tried hard as I stood there on the level of Roman London, thirty feet below the London of to-day, to picture this spot in its glory. It was

The Heart of London

no doubt tiled with veined marble, and the London spring water ran in over marble, and the roof perhaps held frescoes showing nymphs and fauns and Pan playing his pipes.

Signor Matania, the artist, has made a fine picture of this bath as he thinks it was when Roman ladies came there to swim without bathing costumes. A pretty picture, but—was the water ever deep enough ?

" Some think it was a hot bath, and some think it was a cold one," said the guide, " but nobody knows. Perhaps we shall know when Mr. Bickford digs underneath, as he wants to do, in search of the heating system."

*   *   *

I climbed up out of Roman London, and a few steps took me to the sight of Bush House and omnibuses racing past to Charing Cross.

Left Behind

"WHAT is the strangest thing a Londoner has lost?" I asked an official of the Lost Property Office in Scotland Yard.

"Well, let's see. Two leg bones came in last week. They had obviously been left in a tramcar by a medical student. Once we had somebody's appendix in oil; but I think the funniest thing I ever remember a man losing—and I've been here thirty-three years—was a tree-climbing bear! Alive? I should say he was alive! You ought to have seen him climb up to the mantelshelf. It turned out that he had been left in a cab by a Scotsman who owned him. This man had been abroad for a long time, and was paying his first visit to London after many seafaring years abroad. Apparently he was so excited to be back that he forgot all about his bear. He left it in a four-wheeler. He remembered next morning, and jolly glad we were, too, for although we get all kinds of strange things in this department it's not organized like a zoo."

During thirty-three years in the Lost Property Office this official has seen a great change in London's crop of forgetfulness.

"Muffs have stopped coming in now," he said. "Once we were full of muffs; but women don't carry them nowadays. Everything else has increased, not because people are more absent-minded, but because the speed of traffic has increased. We take only objects found in omnibuses, tramcars, and taxicabs. In the old days you could run after a horse omnibus and find your umbrella, but to-day as soon as you remember you have left it the vehicle is out of sight. Just look here!"

We walked down a long avenue packed with umbrellas. There must have been over twenty thousand of them! The avenue ended in a room full of the more recently abandoned specimens. Here men and women were nosing round looking for their lost property. What a task! The room was stacked to the ceiling with umbrellas, all neatly docketed. They lay in racks, the handles only protruding.

When handles are round and shiny this room, which is always full, presents to the eye four walls of round and shiny knobs; when the fashion in umbrellas changes, this room changes too. At the moment it is full of originality and colour. Thousands of green jade and red coral handles jut from the walls; thousands of check handles vary the pattern. Here and there you see a dog-headed handle, a handle shaped like a bird, or a handle carved to the shape of a pierrot's head, a pathetic white face with drooping carmine lips, which seems crying to be claimed and taken home!

"Oh, I shall never find it in this forest of umbrellas!" cried a girl. "Never! I don't think I want to. I hate the look of umbrellas."

Another woman picked her umbrella out in the first five minutes. What an eye! And all the

Left Behind

time girls came up to the counter, rather breathless, with :

" I've lost a lovely new umbrella on a number three omnibus ; it had a dear little green handle carved like a fish, and I said to mother——"

" Come inside, miss," said a weary official.

" I said to mother that I think I lost it when I got off at Westminster, or it may have been earlier in the morning, when——"

" Come inside, miss ! "

More remarkable even than the jungle of lost umbrellas is the series of rooms packed with every conceivable thing a passenger can carry in a tramcar, an omnibus, or a taxicab. You gain the impression when you tour the Lost Property Office that some people would lose an elephant between Ludgate Circus and Charing Cross.

How do they lose full-size typewriters, gigantic suit-cases packed with clothes, gramophones, bulky parcels, crates, and small perambulators ?

There are thousands of lost shoes, mostly new, some of them dance slippers bought by forgetful girls, or perhaps by husbands who were thinking of something else ! There are ball dresses that have been left in omnibuses, silk nightdresses, hats, costumes, and, of course, jewellery.

The Lost Property Office looks like a gigantic pawnshop or a large secondhand store. The officials are surprised at nothing. Have they not taken care of skulls and the hands of mummies ?

In another room I saw October's crop of lost umbrellas being distributed to the tramcar conductors, the omnibus conductors, and the taxicab men who found them. This happens every three months. If it did not Scotland Yard would have to build an annexe somewhere. The finders made merry as they were given incongruous umbrellas. One large, red taxicab driver drew a neat little mincing silk umbrella with a kingfisher on the handle.

" Oh, how sweet, Bill ! " said the tram conductors.

* * *

At the other end of the office other conductors were handing in dozens of umbrellas and sticks, the ceaseless daily harvest of London's wonderful absent-mindedness. Most of them had wrist straps, too !

The " Girls " ∘ ∘ ∘ ∘ ∘

EVEN as I write Piccadilly is changing.
Eros, attended by the ghosts of under-
graduates, has stepped from the pinnacle, thus
evacuating the post of honour from which he has
gazed upon the follies of our fathers, those wicked
men who used to wait outside stage doors with
bouquets before sneaking off somewhere to dine
with a real actress. Ah, those must have been
good days. . . .

So before the circle is squared, which seems
quite unnatural, I wish to write about the flower
" girls." Early in the morning, long before the
first pair of silk stockings had been sold in Regent
Street, the " girls " dipped their violets in the
Fountain and camped out on the steps. What a
perfect picture they made. It always seemed to
me that some unknown admirer of Phil May was
secretly subsidizing them, paying for them, working, maybe, to stamp on the national mind a sharp
memory of plaid shawls tight over plump shoulders,
apple-red faces beneath black straw hats. In the
spring they brought the first real news to the
West End with their laughing primroses, big tight
gold bunches of them ; and the Fountain was a
joy to behold.

" Vi'lets pennigabunch."

That was, of course, long ago. I believe they
are sixpence or more now ; but the old cry
from the Fountain has been remembered all

over the earth wherever men have thought of Piccadilly.

The flower " girls " of Piccadilly presented to London the most marvellous study in polite indifference. Here they were in occupation of the very centre of the world with the feminine beauty and elegance of every country always before their eyes. They remained unaffected. They were the only women in London moving in fashionable London circles who did not care a hang for the changing mode. They had sold violets to women in bustles ; they had seen skirts sweep the ground, they had seen the dawn of the leg, from the hobble skirt to the knee skirt. Never once in their history did they show the instinct of their sex to imitate.

These middle-aged women who are always " girls " have become international. American women said : " Why, they're just sweet," French-women thought they were almost chic, and some-times a grey old man, sickened by the degeneracy of these times, would wander up from the direction of Pall Mall to buy a buttonhole just to hear himself called " dearie," and to know that there was still something in London that had not changed. They were Victorian London.

When I heard that Eros was to disappear and that the " girls " were to be moved away I had the same kind of shock that a Roman under the Empire might have suffered if a friend had moved his thumb in the direction of the Palatine Hill and had remarked : " Have you heard ? The Old Man's sacked the Vestal Virgins ! "

The " Girls "

Preposterous! The "girls" *were* our vestal virgins—they kindled each day memory of a fast-vanishing London.

* * *

I found one in Piccadilly the other day. She had taken up a stand on a street refuge, from which she could command sight of her former pitch.

"No, dearie," she said. "Piccadilly's gorn to the dorgs, strite it 'as. Life ain't what it was, nor never will be agin with this squarin' of a plice what was meant to be a circus. It ain't right. Who'd 'ave thought we should leave the Fountain —ever. Some say we can go beck there when they've done messin' it about, but I don't believe it. I'm Mrs. Wise I'm am. There ain't no green in my eye. . . .

"And this job ain't what it once was—not by half. No, dearie! In the old days every kebbie had his buttonhole, and no gent was dressed unless he had one too. And the drivers of the old horse omnibuses! They were rare customers—nice, pleasant men, too, who liked to pass the time of day with you and talk. Now there's no time for talk or flowers."

She nodded enigmatically.

"Young men don't like to be seen carrying flowers to-day, but I can tell you their fathers didn't mind—and better men they were, if I'm any judge of a man, and I ought to be, seeing I've been sat in Piccadilly Circus all me life. . . ."

The Heart of London

Then she said something that sent a chill to my heart :

" My gels ain't going to waste their lives sitting here, I can tell you. Emma going into pickles, and Maud, she's in millinery."

This, of course, is the end ! A flower girl's calling is hereditary. It descends through the distaff side. The next generation of " girls " are, it appears, going into commerce, and there will be none to follow on.

It is sad. If I were a millionaire I would subsidize them and buy a hansom cab and an old pensioned cab-horse to stand there too.

*　　*　　*

For in the fret and change of these days the flower " girls " of Piccadilly looked so permanent with the surge of London round them, the crowds from the ends of the earth, so indifferent to change, so typical of an easier day, as they sold their flowers in that whirl of gladness and sadness, beauty and ugliness, which is the heart of London : : : the heart of the world.

PRINTED BY
JARROLD AND SONS LTD.
NORWICH

METHUEN'S GENERAL LITERATURE

A SELECTION OF

Messrs. Methuen's PUBLICATIONS

This Catalogue contains only a selection of the more important books published by Messrs. Methuen. A complete catalogue of their publications may be obtained on application.

ARMSTRONG (Anthony).
Two Legs and Four. Illustrated by René Bull. 5s. net.
Livestock in Barracks. Illustrated by E. H. Shepard. 6s. net.
Warriors at Ease.   Warriors still at Ease.
Percival and I.   Percival at Play.
How to do It.   Me and Frances.
                    Each 3s. 6d. net.

BAIN (F. W.).
In the Great God's Hair.   A Draught of the Blue.
An Incarnation of the Snow   A Mine of Faults.
A Digit of the Moon.   The Livery of Eve.
A Heifer of the Dawn.   An Essence of the Dusk.
The Descent of the Sun.   The Ashes of a God.
Bubbles of the Foam.   A Syrup of the Bees.
            The Substance of a Dream.
                    Each 3s. 6d. net.

BELLOC (H.).
A History of England. In Five Volumes. Vols. I, II and III. Each 15s. net.
Marie Antoinette. Illustrated. 18s. net.
Paris. Illustrated. 8s. 6d. net.
The Pyrenees. Illustrated. 8s. 6d. net.
On Nothing.   Hills and the Sea.
On Something.   First and Last.
On.   This and That.
On Anything.   On Everything.
Emmanual Burden.   A Picked Company.
                    Each 3s. 6d. net.

BIRMINGHAM (George A.).
A Wayfarer in Hungary. Illustrated. 8s. 6d. net.
Spillikins.   Ships and Sealing-Wax.
        Two Volumes of Essays. Each 3s. 6d. net.

CHESTERTON (G. K.).

COME TO THINK OF IT . . .   6s. net.
G. K. C. AS M.C.   Edited by J. P. DE FONSEKA.   7s. 6d. net.
GENERALLY SPEAKING.   CHARLES DICKENS.
THE OUTLINE OF SANITY.   ALL THINGS CONSIDERED.
TREMENDOUS TRIFLES.   FANCIES VERSUS FADS.
A MISCELLANY OF MEN.   THE FLYING INN.
ALARMS AND DISCURSIONS.   THE USES OF DIVERSITY.
            THE BALLAD OF THE WHITE HORSE.
                        Each 3s. 6d. net.
WINE, WATER AND SONG.   1s. 6d. net.

EINSTEIN (Albert).

RELATIVITY : THE SPECIAL AND GENERAL THEORY.   5s. net.
SIDELIGHTS ON RELATIVITY.   3s. 6d. net.
THE MEANING OF RELATIVITY.   5s. net.
THE BROWNIAN MOVEMENT.   5s. net.

EISLER (Robert).

THE MESSIAH JESUS AND JOHN THE BAPTIST.   According to Flavius
Josephus' recently rediscovered " Capture of Jerusalem " and the
other Jewish and Christian sources.   Illustrated.   £2 2s. net.

FIELD (G. C.).

MORAL THEORY : An Introduction to Ethics.   6s. net.
PLATO AND HIS CONTEMPORARIES.   12s. 6d. net.

FYLEMAN (Rose).

FAIRIES AND CHIMNEYS.   *Twenty-first Edition.*
THE FAIRY GREEN.   *Thirteenth Edition.*
THE FAIRY FLUTE.   *Tenth Edition.*
FAIRIES AND FRIENDS.   THE RAINBOW CAT.
FORTY GOOD-NIGHT TALES.   THE ADVENTURE CLUB.
FORTY GOOD-MORNING TALES.   TWENTY TEA-TIME TALES.
            EIGHT LITTLE PLAYS FOR CHILDREN.
            SEVEN LITTLE PLAYS FOR CHILDREN.
                        Each 3s. 6d. net.
THE DOLLS' HOUSE.   Illustrated.   5s. net.
A GARLAND OF ROSE'S: Collected Poems.   Illustrated.   8s. 6d. net.
GAY GO UP.   Illustrated.   5s. net.
A PRINCESS COMES TO OUR TOWN.   Illustrated.   5s. net.

GIBBON (Edward).

THE DECLINE AND FALL OF THE ROMAN EMPIRE.   Edited, with Notes,
Appendixes, and Maps, by J. B. BURY.   Illustrated.   Seven Volumes.
Each 15s. net.   Also, unillustrated.   Seven Volumes.   Each 7s. 6d. net.

GLOVER (T. R.).

THE CONFLICT OF RELIGIONS IN THE EARLY ROMAN EMPIRE.   10s. 6d.
net.
POETS AND PURITANS.   10s. 6d. net.
VIRGIL.   10s. 6d. net.
FROM PERICLES TO PHILIP.   12s. 6d. net.

GRAHAME (Kenneth).

THE WIND IN THE WILLOWS.   *Thirty-sixth Edition.*   7s. 6d. net.   Also
Pocket Edition, 3s. 6d. net.   Leather, 7s. 6d. net.   Also illustrated by
WYNDHAM PAYNE.   7s. 6d. net.   See also Milne (A. A.).

HADFIELD (J. A.).

PSYCHOLOGY AND MORALS.   6s. net.

HALL (H. R.).

    THE ANCIENT HISTORY OF THE NEAR EAST. Illustrated. £1 1s. net.
    THE CIVILIZATION OF GREECE IN THE BRONZE AGE. Illustrated.
    £1 10s. net.
    A SEASON'S WORK AT UR OF THE CHALDEES. Illustrated. £1 5s. net.

HEATON (Rose Henniker).

    THE PERFECT HOSTESS. Decorated by ALFRED E. TAYLOR. 7s. 6d. net.
    Also special de luxe edition, £1 1s. net.

HERBERT (A. P.).

    TANTIVY TOWERS. 2s. 6d. net.
    WISDOM FOR THE WISE. 5s. net.
    HONEYBUBBLE & CO. 6s. net.
    MISLEADING CASES IN THE COMMON LAW. 5s. net.
    MORE MISLEADING CASES. 5s. net.
    THE BOMBER GIPSY. 3s. 6d. net.
    THE WHEREFORE AND THE WHY. Illustrated. 3s. 6d. net.
    THE SECRET BATTLE. 3s. 6d. net.

HOLDSWORTH (Sir W. S.).

    A HISTORY OF ENGLISH LAW. In Nine Volumes. £1 5s. net each.

HUTTON (Edward).

    CITIES OF SICILY. Illustrated. 10s. 6d. net.
    MILAN AND LOMBARDY.
    THE CITIES OF ROMAGNA AND THE MARCHES.
    SIENA AND SOUTHERN TUSCANY. NAPLES AND SOUTHERN ITALY.
        Each illustrated '8s. 6d. net.
    THE CITIES OF UMBRIA.   THE CITIES OF SPAIN.
    VENICE AND VENETIA.   A WAYFARER IN UNKNOWN TUSCANY.
    FLORENCE AND NORTHERN TUSCANY.   ROME.
    COUNTRY WALKS ABOUT FLORENCE.
        Each illustrated. 7s. 6d. net.

INGE (W. R.), Dean of St. Paul's.

    CHRISTIAN MYSTICISM (The Bampton Lectures for 1899). 7s. 6d. net.

JOHNS (Rowland).

    LET'S TALK OF DOGS.   ALL SORTS OF DOGS.
        Each illustrated. 6s. net.
    DOGS YOU'D LIKE TO MEET.   LET DOGS DELIGHT.
        Each illustrated. 3s. 6d. net.
    PUPPIES. Illustrated. 10s. 6d. net.

KENDRICK (T. D.).

    A HISTORY OF THE VIKINGS. Illustrated. 18s. net.
    THE AXE AGE. Illustrated. 6s. net.
    THE DRUIDS. Illustrated. 12s. 6d. net.
    THE ARCHAEOLOGY OF THE CHANNEL ISLANDS. Vol. I. The Bailiwick
    of Guernsey. Illustrated. £1 5s. net.

KIPLING (Rudyard).

    BARRACK-ROOM BALLADS.   *255th Thousand.*
    THE SEVEN SEAS.   *186th Thousand.*
    THE FIVE NATIONS.   *143rd Thousand.*
    DEPARTMENTAL DITTIES.   *117th Thousand.*
    THE YEARS BETWEEN.   *95th Thousand.*
    Four Editions of these famous volumes of poems are now issued, viz.:
    Crown 8vo, Buckram, 7s. 6d. net. F'cap. 8vo, Cloth, 6s. net. Leather,
    7s. 6d. net. Service Edition.—Two vols. each book. Square F'cap.
    8vo. 3s. net each vol.; and 6s. net.
    TWENTY POEMS. *486th Thousand.* 1s. net.
    A CHOICE OF SONGS. 2s. net.
    A KIPLING ANTHOLOGY—VERSE. Cloth, 6s. net and 3s. 6d. net.
    Leather, 7s. 6d. net.

KNOX (E. V.) ("Evoe").

 THINGS THAT ANNOY ME. PARODIES REGAINED.
     Each 5s. net.
 THESE LIBERTIES. 4s. 6d. net.
 FANCY NOW!   HERE'S MISERY!
 QUAINT SPECIMENS. FICTION AS SHE IS WROTE.
    MR. PUNCH ON THE LINKS.
     Each 6s. net.
 AWFUL OCCASIONS. GORGEOUS TIMES.
 IT OCCURS TO ME.   WONDERFUL OUTINGS.
    THIS OTHER EDEN.
     Each 3s. 6d. net.

LAMB (Charles and Mary).

 THE COMPLETE WORKS. Edited by E. V. LUCAS. Six Volumes. 6s.
  net each. The volumes are :
  1. MISCELLANEOUS PROSE. 3. BOOKS FOR CHILDREN.
  2. ELIA AND THE LAST ESSAYS 4. PLAYS AND POEMS.
   OF ELIA.   5 and 6. LETTERS.
 SELECTED LETTERS. Edited by G. T. CLAPTON. 3s. 6d. net.
 THE CHARLES LAMB DAY BOOK. Compiled by E. V. LUCAS. 6s. net.

LANKESTER (Sir Ray).

 SCIENCE FROM AN EASY CHAIR.
 SCIENCE FROM AN EASY CHAIR (Second Series).
 DIVERSIONS OF A NATURALIST. GREAT AND SMALL THINGS.
     Each illustrated. 7s. 6d. net.
 SECRETS OF EARTH AND SEA. Illustrated. 8s. 6d. net.

LAUGHLIN (Clara E.).

 SO YOU'RE GOING TO GERMANY AND AUSTRIA!
 SO YOU'RE GOING TO SPAIN ! SO YOU'RE GOING TO FRANCE!
 SO YOU'RE GOING TO PARIS! SO YOU'RE GOING TO ROME!
 SO YOU'RE GOING TO ITALY ! SO YOU'RE GOING TO ENGLAND!
    Each illustrated. 10s. 6d. net.
 WHERE IT ALL COMES TRUE IN ITALY AND SWITZERLAND. Illustrated.
 7s. 6d. net.

LINDRUM (Walter).

 BILLIARDS. Illustrated. 6s. net.

LODGE (Sir Oliver).

 MAN AND THE UNIVERSE. 7s. 6d. net and 3s. 6d. net.
 THE SURVIVAL OF MAN. 7s. 6d. net.
 RAYMOND. 10s. 6d. net.
 RAYMOND REVISED. 6s. net.
 MODERN PROBLEMS. 3s. 6d. net.
 REASON AND BELIEF. 3s. 6d. net.
 THE SUBSTANCE OF FAITH. 2s. net.
 RELATIVITY. 1s. net.
 CONVICTION OF SURVIVAL. 2s. net.

LUCAS (E. V.).

 THE LIFE OF CHARLES LAMB. Two Volumes. £1 1s. net
 THE COLVINS AND THEIR FRIENDS. £1 1s. net.
 VERMEER THE MAGICAL. 5s. net.
 A WANDERER IN ROME. 10s. 6d. net.
 A WANDERER IN HOLLAND. 10s. 6d. net.
 A WANDERER IN LONDON. 10s. 6d. net.
 LONDON REVISITED (Revised). 10s. 6d. net.
 A WANDERER IN PARIS. 10s. 6d. net.
 A WANDERER IN FLORENCE. 10s. 6d. net.
 A WANDERER IN VENICE. 10s. 6d. net.
 A WANDERER AMONG PICTURES. 8s. 6d. net.

LUCAS (E. V.)—contd.

E. V. LUCAS'S LONDON. £1 net.
THE OPEN ROAD. 6s. net. India Paper, Leather, 7s. 6d. net.
    Illustrated by CLAUDE A. SHEPPERSON. 10s. 6d. net.
THE JOY OF LIFE. Cloth. 6s. net.
    Leather, 7s. 6d. net. India Paper, Leather, 7s. 6d. net.

FIRESIDE AND SUNSHINE.	THE SECOND POST.
CHARACTER AND COMEDY.	GOOD COMPANY.
ONE DAY AND ANOTHER.	A FRONDED ISLE.
LOITERER'S HARVEST.	OLD LAMPS FOR NEW.
EVENTS AND EMBROIDERIES.	LUCK OF THE YEAR.
THE GENTLEST ART.	A ROVER I WOULD BE.
GIVING AND RECEIVING.	HER INFINITE VARIETY.
ENCOUNTERS AND DIVERSIONS.	TURNING THINGS OVER.

Each 3s. 6d. net.

A BOSWELL OF BAGHDAD.	'TWIXT EAGLE AND DOVE.
THE PHANTOM JOURNAL.	ZIGZAGS IN FRANCE.
CLOUD AND SILVER.	TRAVELLER'S LUCK.

Each 6s. net.
FRENCH LEAVES. Illustrated. 5s. net.

" THE MORE I SEE OF MEN . . ."	IF DOGS COULD WRITE.
OUT OF A CLEAR SKY.	" . . . AND SUCH SMALL DEER."

Each 3s. 6d. net.

THE PEKINESE NATIONAL ANTHEM. Illustrated. 1s. net.
    See also Lamb (C. and M.)

LYND (Robert).

THE BLUE LION.	THE PEAL OF BELLS.
THE MONEY-BOX.	THE ORANGE TREE.
THE LITTLE ANGEL.	THE GOLDFISH.
THE GREEN MAN.	THE PLEASURES OF IGNORANCE.

Each 3s. 6d. net.
IT'S A FINE WORLD. 5s. net.

McDOUGALL (William).

AN INTRODUCTION TO SOCIAL PSYCHOLOGY. 10s. 6d. net.
BODY AND MIND. 12s. 6d. net.
AN OUTLINE OF PSYCHOLOGY. 10s. 6d. net.
NATIONAL WELFARE AND DECAY. 6s. net.
ETHICS AND SOME MODERN WORLD PROBLEMS. 7s. 6d. net.
AN OUTLINE OF ABNORMAL PSYCHOLOGY. 15s. net.
CHARACTER AND THE CONDUCT OF LIFE. 10s. 6d. net.
MODERN MATERIALISM AND EMERGENT EVOLUTION. 7s. 6d. net.

MAETERLINCK (Maurice).

THE BLUE BIRD. 6s. net and 2s. 6d. net.
THE BETROTHAL. 6s. net and 3s. 6d. net.
DEATH. 3s. 6d. net.
OUR ETERNITY. 6s. net.
THE UNKNOWN GUEST. 6s. net.

MALLET (Sir C. E.).

A HISTORY OF THE UNIVERSITY OF OXFORD. Three Volumes. Illustrated. Each £1 1s. net.

MARLOWE (Christopher).

The Works of. In 6 Vols. General Editor, R. H. CASE.
    I. LIFE OF MARLOWE; AND DIDO, QUEEN OF CARTHAGE. By C. F. TUCKER BROOKE. 8s. 6d. net.
    II. TAMBURLAINE THE GREAT. By U. M. ELLIS-FERMOR. 10s. 6d. net.
    III THE JEW OF MALTA and THE MASSACRE AT PARIS. By H. S. BENNETT. 10s. 6d. net

METHUEN (Sir A.).
AN ANTHOLOGY OF MODERN VERSE. 232nd *Thousand.*
SHAKESPEARE TO HARDY: An Anthology of English Lyrics. 28th
Thousand.
Each, Cloth, 6s. net. Leather, 7s. 6d. net.

MILNE (A. A.).
THOSE WERE THE DAYS. 7s. 6d. net.
TOAD OF TOAD HALL. A Play from Kenneth Grahame's " THE WIND
IN THE WILLOWS." 5s. net.
BY WAY OF INTRODUCTION. 6s. net.
NOT THAT IT MATTERS.   IF I MAY.
THE DAY'S PLAY.   THE HOLIDAY ROUND.
ONCE A WEEK.   THE SUNNY SIDE.
Each 3s. 6d. net.
WHEN WE WERE VERY YOUNG.   211th *Thousand.*
WINNIE-THE-POOH.   118th *Thousand.*
NOW WE ARE SIX.   119th *Thousand.*
THE HOUSE AT POOH CORNER.   105th *Thousand.*
Each illustrated by E. H. SHEPARD. 7s. 6d. net. Leather, 10s. 6d. net.
THE CHRISTOPHER ROBIN STORY BOOK. Illustrated by E. H. SHEPARD.
5s. net.
THE CHRISTOPHER ROBIN BIRTHDAY BOOK. Illustrated by E. H.
SHEPARD. 3s. 6d. net.
FOR THE LUNCHEON INTERVAL. 1s. 6d. net.

MORTON (H. V.).
THE HEART OF LONDON. 35th *Thousand.* 3s. 6d. net. Also, Illustrated
by L. Hummel. 6s. net.
THE SPELL OF LONDON. 25th *Thousand.* 3s. 6d. net.
THE NIGHTS OF LONDON. 18th *Thousand.* 3s. 6d. net.

IN SEARCH OF ENGLAND. 84th *Thousand.*
THE CALL OF ENGLAND. 36th *Thousand.*
IN SEARCH OF SCOTLAND. 106th *Thousand.*
IN SEARCH OF IRELAND. 40th *Thousand.*
Each illustrated. 7s. 6d. net.

PETRIE (Sir Flinders).
A HISTORY OF EGYPT. Illustrated. Six Volumes.
1. FROM THE 1ST TO XVITH DYNASTY (12s. net). 2. THE XVIITH
AND XVIIITH DYNASTIES (9s. net). 3. XIXTH TO XXXTH DYNASTIES
(12s. net). 4. PTOLEMAIC EGYPT. EDWYN BEVAN. (15s. net.) 5.
EGYPT UNDER ROMAN RULE. J. G. MILNE. (12s. net.) 6. EGYPT
IN THE MIDDLE AGES. STANLEY LANE-POOLE. (10s. net.)

RICHARDSON (T. D.).
MODERN FIGURE SKATING. Illustrated. 15s. net.

RUTTER (Frank).
EL GRECO. Illustrated. £1 10s. net.

SELLAR (W. C.) and YEATMAN (R. J.).
1066 AND ALL THAT. A comic history. Illustrated by JOHN REY-
NOLDS. 50th *Thousand.* 5s. net.

SOMERVELL (D. C.).
ENGLISH THOUGHT IN THE NINETEENTH CENTURY. 6s. net.

TILDEN (William T.).
THE ART OF LAWN TENNIS (Revised Edition).
SINGLES AND DOUBLES.
Each illustrated. 6s. net.
LAWN TENNIS FOR YOUNG PLAYERS.
LAWN TENNIS FOR CLUB PLAYERS.
LAWN TENNIS FOR MATCH PLAYERS.
Each illustrated. 2s. 6d. net.

TILDEN (William T.)—contd.

THE COMMON SENSE OF LAWN TENNIS.
MATCH PLAY AND THE SPIN OF THE BALL.
Each illustrated. 5s. net.
ME—THE HANDICAP. 5s. net.

UNDERHILL (Evelyn).

MYSTICISM. (Revised Edition.) 15s. net.
THE LIFE OF THE SPIRIT AND THE LIFE OF TO-DAY. 7s. 6d. net.
CONCERNING THE INNER LIFE. THE HOUSE OF THE SOUL.
Each 2s. net.
MAN AND THE SUPERNATURAL. 7s. 6d. net.

VARDON (Harry).

HOW TO PLAY GOLF. Illustrated. 19th Edition. 5s. net.
THE COMPLETE GOLFER. Illustrated. 21st Edition. 12s. 6d. net.

WARD (A. C.).

TWENTIETH-CENTURY LITERATURE. 5s. net.
THE NINETEEN-TWENTIES. 5s. net.

WILDE (Oscar).

THE WORKS OF OSCAR WILDE. Sixteen Volumes. Each 6s. 6d. net.
Some also 2s. 6d. net.
1. LORD ARTHUR SAVILE'S CRIME AND THE PORTRAIT OF MR. W. H.
2. THE DUCHESS OF PADUA. 3. POEMS. 4. LADY WINDERMERE'S FAN.
5. A WOMAN OF NO IMPORTANCE. 6. AN IDEAL HUSBAND. 7. THE
IMPORTANCE OF BEING EARNEST. 8. A HOUSE OF POMEGRANATES. 9.
INTENTIONS. 10. DE PROFUNDIS AND PRISON LETTERS. 11. ESSAYS.
12. SALOME, A FLORENTINE TRAGEDY, AND LA SAINTE COURTISANE.
14. SELECTED PROSE OF OSCAR WILDE. 15. ART AND DECORATION.
16. FOR LOVE OF THE KING: A Burmese Masque (5s. net). 17. VERA,
OR THE NIHILISTS.